Oracle SQL and PL/SQL

Solved SQL and PL/SQL Questions and Answers

Including

Queries and Tips

With

80 Frequently Asked SQL Questions and Answers

60 Frequently Asked PL/SQL Questions and Answers

Solved 51 Frequently Asked Basic SQL Queries

Solved 25 Frequently Asked Complex SQL Queries

Top 120 SQL and PL/SQL Tips

(Author- Niraj Gupta)

Table of Contents

Best 80 SQL Questions and Answers 3

Best 60 PL/SQL Questions and Answers 28

Best 51 Solved Basic SQL Queries 45

Best 25 Solved Advanced SQL Queries 58

Best 120 SQL and PL/SQL Tips...76

Best 80 SQL Questions and Answers

Question 1: What is SQL and also describe types of SQL statements?

SQL stands for Structured Query Language. SQL is a language used to communicate with the server to access, manipulate and control data.

There are 5 different types of SQL statements.

1) Data Retrieval: SELECT

2) Data Manipulation Language (DML): INSERT, UPDATE, DELETE, MERGE

3) Data Definition Language (DDL): CREATE, ALTER, DROP, RENAME, TRUNCATE.

4) Transaction Control Statements: COMMIT, ROLLBACK, SAVEPOINT

5) Data Control Language (DCL): GRANT, REVOKE

Question 2: What is an alias in SQL statements?

Alias is a user-defined alternative name given to the column or table. By default column alias headings appear in upper case. Enclose the alias in a double quotation marks (" ") to make it case sensitive. "**AS**" Keyword before the alias name makes the SELECT clause easier to read.

For ex: Select empname AS name from employee; (Here AS is a keyword and "name" is an alias).

Question 3: What is a Literal? Give an example where it can be used?

A Literal is a string that can contain a character, a number, or a date that is included in the SELECT list and that is not a column name or a column alias. Date and character literals must be enclosed within single quotation marks (' '), number literals need not.

For ex: Select last_name||'is a'||job_id As "emp details" from employee; (Here "is a" is a literal).

Question 4: What is a difference between SQL and iSQL*Plus?

SQL	iSQL*Plus

Is a Language	Is an Environment
Character and date columns heading are left-justified and number column headings are right-justified.	Default heading justification is in Centre.
Cannot be Abbreviated (short forms)	Can be Abbreviated
Does not have a continuation character	Has a dash (-) as a continuation character if the command is longer than one line
Use Functions to perform some formatting	Use commands to format data

Question 5: Define the order of Precedence used in executing SQL statements.

Order Evaluated	Operator
1	Arithmetic operators (*, /, +, -)
2	Concatenation operators (||)
3	Comparison conditions
4	Is[NOT] NULL, LIKE, [NOT] IN
5	[NOT] BETWEEN
6	NOT Logical condition
7	AND logical condition
8	OR logical condition

Question 6: What are SQL functions? Describe in brief different types of SQL functions?

SQL Functions are very powerful feature of SQL. SQL functions can take arguments but always return some value.

There are two distinct types of SQL functions:

1) **Single-Row functions:** These functions operate on a single row to give one result per row.

Types of Single-Row functions:

1) Character

2) Number

3) Date

4) Conversion

5) General

2) **Multiple-Row functions:** These functions operate on groups of rows to give one result per group of rows.

Types of Multiple-Row functions:

1) AVG

2) COUNT

3) MAX

4) MIN

5) SUM

6) STDDEV

7) VARIANCE

Question 7: Explain character, number and date function in detail?

Character functions: accept character input and return both character and number values. Types of character function are:

a) Case-Manipulation Functions: LOWER, UPPER, INITCAP

b) Character-Manipulation Functions: CONCAT, SUBSTR, LENGTH, INSTR, LPAD/RPAD, TRIM, REPLACE

Number Functions: accept Numeric input and return numeric values. Number Functions are: ROUND, TRUNC and MOD

Date Functions: operates on values of the Date data type. (All date functions return a value of DATE data type except the MONTHS_BETWEEN Function, which returns a number. Date Functions are MONTHS_BETWEEN, ADD_MONTHS, NEXT_DAY, LAST_DAY, ROUND, TRUNC.

Question 8: What is a Dual Table?

Dual table is owned by the user SYS and can be accessed by all users. It contains one column **Dummy** and one row with the value **X.** The Dual Table is useful when you want to return a value only once. The value can be a constant, pseudocolumn or expression that is not derived from a table with user data.

Question 9: Explain Conversion function in detail?

Conversion Functions converts a value from one data type to another. Conversion functions are of two types:

Implicit Data type conversion:

1)   VARCHAR2 or CHAR To NUMBER, DATE

2)   NUMBER To VARCHAR2

3)   DATE To VARCHAR2

Explicit data type conversion:

1)   TO_NUMBER

2)   TO_CHAR

3)   TO_DATE

TO_NUMBER function is used to convert Character string to Number format. TO_NUMBER function use fx modifier. Format: TO_NUMBER (char[, ' format_model']). fx modifier specifies the exact matching for the character argument and number format model of TO_NUMBER function.

TO_CHAR function is used to convert NUMBER or DATE data type to CHARACTER format. TO_CHAR Function use fm element to remove padded blanks or suppress leading zeros. TO_CHAR Function formats:TO_CHAR (date, 'format_model').Format model must be enclosed in single quotation marks and is case sensitive.

For ex: Select TO_CHAR (hiredate, 'MM/YY') from employee.

TO_DATE function is used to convert Character string to date format. TO_DATE function use fx modifier which specifies the exact matching for the character argument and date format model of TO_DATE function. TO_DATE function format: TO_DATE (char[, ' format_model']).

For ex: Select TO_DATE ('may 24 2007','mon dd rr') from dual;

Question 10: Describe different types of General Function used in SQL?

General functions are of following types:

1) NVL: Converts a null value to an actual value. NVL (exp1, exp2) .If exp1 is null then NVL function return value of exp2.

2) NVL2: If exp1 is not null, nvl2 returns exp2, if exp1 is null, nvl2 returns exp3. The argument exp1 can have any data type. NVL2 (exp1, exp2, exp3)

3) NULLIF: Compares two expressions and returns null if they are equal or the first expression if they are not equal. NULLIF (exp1, exp2)

4) COALESCE: Returns the first non-null expression in the expression list. COALESCE (exp1, exp2... expn). The advantage of the COALESCE function over NVL function is that the COALESCE function can take multiple alternative values.

5) Conditional Expressions: Provide the use of IF-THEN-ELSE logic within a SQL statement. Example: CASE Expression and DECODE Function.

Question 11: What is difference between COUNT (*), COUNT (expression), COUNT (distinct expression)? (Where expression is any column name of Table)

COUNT (*): Returns number of rows in a table including duplicates rows and rows containing null values in any of the columns.

COUNT (EXP): Returns the number of non-null values in the column identified by expression.

COUNT (DISTINCT EXP): Returns the number of unique, non-null values in the column identified by expression.

Question 12: What is a Sub Query? Describe its Types?

A sub query is a SELECT statement that is embedded in a clause of another SELECT statement. Sub query can be placed in WHERE, HAVING and FROM clause.

Guidelines for using sub queries:

1) Enclose sub queries within parenthesis

2) Place sub queries on the right side of the comparison condition.

3) Use Single-row operators with single-row sub queries and Multiple-row operators with multiple-row sub queries.

Types of sub queries:

1) Single-Row Sub query: Queries that return only one row from the Inner select statement. Single-row comparison operators are: =, >, >=, <, <=, <>

2) Multiple-Row Sub query: Queries that return more than one row from the inner Select statement. There are also multiple-column sub queries that return more than one column from the inner select statement. Operators includes: IN, ANY, ALL.

Question 13: What is difference between ANY and ALL operators?

ANY Operator compares value to each value returned by the subquery. ANY operator has a synonym SOME operator.

> ANY means more than the minimum.

< ANY means less than the maximum

= ANY is equivalent to IN operator.

ALL Operator compares value to every value returned by the subquery.

> ALL means more than the maximum

< ALL means less than the minimum

<> ALL is equivalent to NOT IN condition.

Question 14: What is a MERGE statement?

The MERGE statement inserts or updates rows in one table, using data from another table. It is useful in data warehousing applications.

Question 15: What is a difference between "VERIFY" and "FEEDBACK" command?

VERIFY Command: Use VERIFY Command to confirm the changes in the SQL statement (Old and New values). Defined with SET VERIFY ON/OFF.

Feedback Command: Displays the number of records returned by a query.

Question 16: What is the use of Double Ampersand (&&) in SQL Queries? Give example?

Use "&&" if you want to reuse the variable value without prompting the user each time.

For ex: Select empno, ename, &&column_name from employee order by &column_name;

Question 17: What are Joins and how many types of Joins are there?

Joins are used to retrieve data from more than one table.

There are 5 different types of joins.

Oracle 8i and Prior	SQL: 1999 (9i)
Equi Join	Natural/Inner Join
Outer Join	Left Outer/ Right Outer/ Full Outer Join
Self Join	Join ON
Non-Equi Join	Join USING
Cartesian Product	Cross Join

Question 18: Explain all Joins used in Oracle 8i?

Cartesian Join: When a Join condition is invalid or omitted completely, the result is a Cartesian product, in which all combinations of rows are displayed. To avoid a Cartesian product, always include a valid join condition in a "where" clause. To Join 'N' tables together, you need a minimum of N-1 Join conditions. For ex: to join four tables, a minimum of three joins is required. This rule may not apply if the table has a concatenated primary key, in which case more than one column is required to uniquely identify each row.

Equi Join: This type of Join involves primary and foreign key relation. Equi Join is also called Simple or Inner Joins.

Non-Equi Joins: A Non-Equi Join condition containing something other than an equality operator. The relationship is obtained using an operator other than equal operator (=).The conditions such as <= and >= can be used, but BETWEEN is the simplest to represent Non-Equi Joins.

Outer Joins: Outer Join is used to fetch rows that do not meet the join condition. The outer join operator is the plus sign (+), and it is placed on the side of the join that is deficient in information. The Outer Join operator can appear on only one side of the expression, the side that has information missing. It returns those rows from one table that has no direct match in the other table. A condition involving an Outer Join cannot use IN and OR operator.

Self Join: Joining a table to itself.

Question 19: Explain all Joins used in Oracle 9i and later release?

Cross Join: Cross Join clause produces the cross-product of two tables. This is same as a Cartesian product between the two tables.

Natural Joins: Is used to join two tables automatically based on the columns which have matching data types and names, using the keyword NATURAL JOIN. It is equal to the Equi-Join. If the columns have the same names but different data types, than the Natural Join syntax causes an error.

Join with the USING clause: If several columns have the same names but the data types do not match, than the NATURAL JOIN clause can be modified with the USING clause to specify the columns that should be used for an equi Join. Use the USING clause to match only one column when more than one column matches. Do not use a table name or alias in the referenced columns. The NATURAL JOIN clause and USING clause are mutually exclusive.

For ex: Select a.city, b.dept_name from loc a Join dept b USING (loc_id) where loc_id=10;

Joins with the ON clause: Use the ON clause to specify a join condition. The ON clause makes code easy to understand. ON clause is equals to Self Joins. The ON clause can also be used to join columns that have different names.

Left/ Right/ Full Outer Joins: Left Outer Join displays all rows from the table that is Left to the LEFT OUTER JOIN clause, right outer join displays all rows from the table that is right to the RIGHT OUTER JOIN clause, and full outer join displays all rows from both the tables either left or right to the FULL OUTER JOIN clause.

Question 20: What is a difference between Entity, Attribute and Tuple?

Entity: A significant thing about which some information is required. For ex: EMPLOYEE (table). Attribute: Something that describes the entity. For ex: empno, empname, empaddress (columns). Tuple: A row in a relation is called Tuple.

Question 21: What is a Transaction? Describe common errors can occur while executing any Transaction?

Transaction consists of a collection of DML statements that forms a logical unit of work.

The common errors that can occur while executing any transaction are:

1) The violation of constraints.

2) Data type mismatch.

3) Value too wide to fit in column.

4) The system crashes or Server gets down.

5) The session Killed.

6) Locking take place. Etc.

Question 22: What is locking in SQL? Describe its types?

Locking prevents destructive interaction between concurrent transactions. Locks held until Commit or Rollback. Types of locking are: **Implicit Locking:** Occurs for all SQL statements except SELECT.

Explicit Locking: Can be done by user manually.

Further there are two locking methods:

1) Exclusive: Locks out other users

2) Share: Allows other users to access

Question 23: What is a difference between Commit, Rollback and Savepoint?

COMMIT: Ends the current transaction by making all pending data changes permanent. ROLLBACK: Ends the current transaction by discarding all pending data changes. SAVEPOINT: Divides a transaction into smaller parts. You can rollback the transaction till a particular named savepoint.

Question 24: What are the advantages of COMMIT and ROLLBACK statements?

Advantages of COMMIT and ROLLBACK statements are:

a) Ensure data consistency

b) Can preview data changes before making changes permanent.

c) Group logically related operations.

Question 25: Describe naming rules for creating a Table?

Naming rules to be consider for creating a table are:

1)   Table name must begin with a letter,

2)   Table name can be 1-30 characters long,

3)   Table name can contain only A-Z, a-z, 0-9,_ $, #.

4)   Table name cannot duplicate the name of another object owned by the same user.

5)   Table name cannot be an oracle server reserved word.

Question 26: What is a DEFAULT option in a table?

A column can be given a default value by using the DEFAULT option. This option prevents null values from entering the column if a row is inserted without a value for that column. The DEFAULT value can be a literal, an expression, or a SQL function such as SYSDATE and USER but the value cannot be the name of another column or a pseudo column such as NEXTVAL or CURRVAL.

Question 27: What is a difference between USER TABLES and DATA DICTIONARY?

USER TABLES: Is a collection of tables created and maintained by the user. Contain USER information. DATA DICTIONARY: Is a collection of tables created and maintained by the Oracle Server. It contains database information. All data dictionary tables are owned by the SYS user.

Question 28: Describe few Data Types used in SQL?

Data Types is a specific storage format used to store column values. Few data types used in SQL are:

1)   VARCHAR2(size): Minimum size is '1' and Maximum size is '4000'

2)   CHAR(size): Minimum size is '1'and Maximum size is '2000'

3)   NUMBER(P,S):" Precision" can range from 1 to 38 and the "Scale" can range from

-84 to 127.

4) DATE

5) LONG: 2GB

6) CLOB: 4GB

7) RAW (size): Maximum size is 2000

8) LONG RAW: 2GB

9) BLOB: 4GB

10) BFILE: 4GB

11) ROWID: A 64 base number system representing the unique address of a row in the table.

Question 29: In what scenario you can modify a column in a table?

During modifying a column:

1)   You can increase the width or precision of a numeric column.

2)   You can increase the width of numeric or character columns.

3)   You can decrease the width of a column only if the column contains null values or if the table has no rows.

4)   You can change the data type only if the column contains null values.

5)   You can convert a CHAR column to the VARCHAR2 data type or convert a VARCHAR2 column to the CHAR data type only if the column contains null values or if you do not change the size.

Question 30: Describe few restrictions on using "LONG" data type?

A LONG column is not copied when a table is created using a sub query. A LONG column cannot be included in a GROUP BY or an ORDER BY clause. Only one LONG column can be used per table. No constraint can be defined on a LONG column.

Question 31: What is a SET UNUSED option?

SET UNUSED option marks one or more columns as unused so that they can be dropped when the demand on system resources is lower. Unused columns are treated as if they were dropped, even though their column data remains in the table's rows. After a column has been marked as unused, you have no access to that column. A select * query will not retrieve data from unused columns. In addition, the names and types of columns marked unused will not be displayed during a DESCRIBE, and you can add to the table a new column with the same name as an unused column. The SET UNUSED information is stored in the USER_UNUSED_COL_TABS dictionary view.

Question 32: What is a difference between Truncate and Delete?

The main difference between Truncate and Delete is as below:

TRUNCATE	DELETE
Removes all rows from a table and releases storage space used by that table.	Removes all rows from a table but does not release storage space used by that table.
TRUNCATE Command is faster.	DELETE command is slower.
Is a DDL statement and cannot be Rollback.	Is a DML statement and can be Rollback.
Database Triggers do not fire on TRUNCATE.	Database Triggers fire on DELETE.

Question 33: What is a main difference between CHAR and VARCHAR2?

CHAR pads blank spaces to a maximum length, whereas VARCHAR2 does not pad blank spaces.

Question 34: What are Constraints? How many types of constraints are there?

Constraints are used to prevent invalid data entry or deletion if there are dependencies. Constraints enforce rules at the table level. Constraints can be created either at the same time as the table is created or after the table has been created. Constraints can be defined at the column or table level. Constraint defined for a specific table can be viewed by looking at the USER-CONSTRAINTS data dictionary table. You can define any constraint at the table level except NOT NULL which is defined only at column level. There are 5 types of constraints:

1) Not Null Constraint

2) Unique Key Constraint

3) Primary Key Constraint

4) Foreign Key Constraint

5) Check Key Constraint.

Question 35: Describe types of Constraints in brief?

NOT NULL: NOT NULL Constraint ensures that the column contains no null values.

UNIQUE KEY: UNIQUE Key Constraint ensures that every value in a column or set of columns must be unique, that is, no two rows of a table can have duplicate values in a specified column or set of columns. If the UNIQUE constraint comprises more than one column, that group of columns is called a Composite Unique Key. There can be more than one Unique key on a table. Unique Key Constraint allows the input of Null values. Unique Key automatically creates index on the column it is created.

PRIMARY KEY: Uniquely identifies each row in the Table. Only one PRIMARY KEY can be created for each table but can have several UNIQUE constraints. PRIMARY KEY ensures that no column can contain a NULL value. A Unique Index is automatically created for a PRIMARY KEY column. PRIMARY KEY is called a Parent key.

FOREIGN KEY: Is also called Referential Integrity Constraint. FOREIGN KEY is one in which a column or set of columns take references of the Primary/Unique key of same or another table. FOREIGN KEY is called a child key. A FOREIGN KEY value must match an existing value in the parent table or be null.

CHECK KEY: Defines a condition that each row must satisfy. A single column can have multiple CHECK Constraints. During CHECK constraint following expressions is not allowed:

1)   References to CURRVAL, NEXTVAL, LEVEL and ROWNUM Pseudo columns.

2)   Calls to SYSDATE, UID, USER and USERENV Functions

Question 36: What is the main difference between Unique Key and Primary Key?

The main difference between Unique Key and Primary Key are:

Unique Key	Primary Key
A table can have more than one Unique Key.	A table can have only one Primary Key.
Unique key column can store NULL values.	Primary key column cannot store NULL values.
Uniquely identify each value in a column.	Uniquely identify each row in a table.

Question 37: What is a difference between ON DELETE CASCADE and ON DELETE SET NULL?

ON DELETE CASCADE Indicates that when the row in the parent table is deleted, the dependent rows in the child table will also be deleted. ON DELETE SET NULL Coverts foreign key values to null when the parent value is removed. Without the ON DELETE CASCADE or the ON DELETE SET NULL options, the row in the parent table cannot be deleted if it is referenced in the child table.

Question 38: What is a Candidate Key?

The columns in a table that can act as a Primary Key are called Candidate Key.

Question 39: What are Views and why they are used?

A View logically represents subsets of data from one or more table. A View is a logical table based on a table or another view. A View contains no data of its own but is like a window through which data from tables can be viewed or changed. The tables on which a view is based are called Base Tables. The View is stored as a SELECT statement in the data dictionary. View definitions can be retrieved from the data dictionary table: USER_VIEWS.

Views are used:

1) To restrict data access

2) To make complex queries easy

3) To provide data Independence

4) Views provide groups of user to access data according to their requirement.

Question 40: What is a difference between Simple and Complex Views?

The main differences between two views are:

Simple View	Complex View
Derives data from only one table.	Derives data from many tables.
Contains no functions or group of data	Contain functions or groups of data.
Can perform DML operations through the view.	Does not always allow DML operations through the view.

Question 41: What are the restrictions of DML operations on Views?

Few restrictions of DML operations on Views are:

You cannot DELETE a row if the View contains the following:

1) Group Functions

2) A Group By clause

3) The Distinct Keyword

4) The Pseudo column ROWNUM Keyword.

You cannot MODIFY data in a View if it contains the following:

1) Group Functions

2) A Group By clause

3) The Distinct Keyword

4) The Pseudo column ROWNUM Keyword.

5) Columns defined by expressions (Ex; Salary * 12)

You cannot INSERT data through a view if it contains the following:

1) Group Functions

2) A Group By clause

3) The Distinct Keyword

4) The Pseudo column ROWNUM Keyword.

5) Columns defined by expressions (Ex; Salary * 12)

6) NOT NULL columns in the base tables that are not selected by the View.

Question 42: What is an Inline view?

Inline view is a sub query with an Alias name. I.e. Giving an alias to a sub query written in the FROM clause.

Question 43: What is a Sequence?

Sequence generates primary key values that are unique for each row. A sequence is a user created database objects that can be shared by multiple users to generate unique integers. Sequence saves time and reduces the amount of application code needed. Sequence numbers are stored and generated independently of tables. Therefore, the same sequence can be used for multiple tables. Information about the sequence can be found in the USER_SEQUENCES table of the data dictionary. To use sequence, refer it with either the NEXTVAL or the CURRVAL pseudo columns.

Question 44: What is a difference between NEXTVAL and CURRVAL pseudo columns?

NEXTVAL pseudo column returns the next available sequence value. It returns a unique value every time it is referenced, even for different users. (Retrieve the next number in the sequence by referencing sequence_name.NEXTVAL).

CURRVALpseudo columnreturns the current available sequence value. (Returns the current available number by referencing sequence_name.CURRVAL).

Question 45: What are the rules for using NEXTVAL and CURRVAL pseudo columns?

Rules for using NEXTVAL and CURRVAL pseudo columns are:

You can use NEXTVAL and CURRVAL in the following contexts:

1) The SELECT list of a SELECT statement that is not a part of a sub query.

2) The SELECT list of a sub query in an INSERT statement.

3) The VALUES clause of an INSERT statement.

4) The SET clause of an UPDATE statement.

You cannot use NEXTVAL and CURRVAL in the following contexts:

1) The SELECT list of a VIEW

2) The SELECT statement with GROUP BY, HAVING, or ORDER BY clause.

3) A sub query in a SELECT, DELETE or UPDATE statement.

4) The SELECT statement with the DISTINCT keyword.

5) The DEFAULT expression in a CREATE TABLE or ALTER TABLE statement.

Question 46: What are Indexes? Describe its Types?

Index is a Schema object that is used to improve the performance of some queries. Is used and maintained automatically by the Oracle server. Indexes can be created explicitly or automatically. If you do not have an index on the column, than a full table scan occurs. Indexes are logically and physically independent of the table indexed. This means that they can be created or dropped at any time and have no affect on the base tables or other indexes. When you drop a table, corresponding indexes are also dropped.

There are two types of Indexes:

1)   Unique Index: Is created automatically when you define a primary key or unique key constraint on a table definition.

2)   Non-Unique Index: Which a user can create on columns to speed up access to the rows.

Question 47: When to create an Index and when not?

Create Index:

1)   If a column contains a wide range of values.

2)   If a column contains a large number of NULL values.

3)   When one or more columns are frequently used together in a WHERE clause or a Join condition.

Not to create Index:

1)   When the table is small

2)   The table is updated frequently.

Also, More Indexes on a table does not mean faster queries. Each DML operations that are committed on a table with indexes must be updated. The more indexes you have associated with a table, the more effort the oracle server must make to update all the indexes after a DML operation.

Question 48: What are SYNONYMS?

Synonyms are an alternative name for an object. With Synonyms you can:

1)   Ease referring to a table owned by another user.

2)   Shorten lengthy objects names.

Database Administrators can create Public Synonyms and Users can create Private Synonyms.

Question 49: What is difference between System Security and Database Security?

System Security covers access and use of the database at the system level, such as username and password, the disk space allocated to users, and the system operations that users can perform. Whereas, Database Security covers access and use of the database objects and the actions that those users can have on the objects.

Question 50: What is Schema?

Schema is a collection of objects, such as tables, Views, Sequences etc. The Schema is owned by a database user and has the same name as that of User.

Question 51: What are Privileges?

Privileges are the right to execute particular SQL statements. The DBA is a high-level user with the ability to grant users access to the database and its objects. The users require system privileges to gain access to the database and object privileges to manipulate the content of the objects in the database. Users can also be given the privilege to grant additional privileges to other users or to roles which are named groups of related privileges.

Question 52: What is a Role?

Role is a named group of related privileges. Roles can be granted to the user. This method makes it easier to revoke and maintain privileges. A user can have access to several Roles and several users can be assigned the same Role. Roles are typically created for database application.

Question 53: What is a GRANT option in SQL?

A user can grant any object privilege on any schema object that the user owns, to any other user or role. If the grant includes WITH GRANT OPTION, than the grantee can further grant the object privilege to other users, otherwise, the grantee can use the privileges but cannot grant it to other users. An owner of a table can grant access to all users by using the PUBLIC keyword.

Question 54: What is a REVOKE option in SQL?

The REVOKE statement is used to revoke privileges granted to other users. If the privileges granted to others through the WITH GRANT OPTION clause, it is then also revoked.

Question 55: What is a Database Links?

A Database Links connection allows local users to access data on a remote database. Database dictionary USER_DB_LINKS contains information on links to which a user has access. Privileges cannot be granted on remote objects.

Question 56: What is a difference between UNION and UNION ALL?

UNION returns all distinct rows. Whereas, UNION ALL returns all rows including duplicates.

Question 57: What is a difference between DBMS and RDBMS?

The main difference between DBMS and RDBMS are:

DBMS(Database Management Systems)	**RDBMS**(Relational Database Management System)
Data is stored in the form of rows and columns.	Data is stored in the form of Tables.
Data stored is temporarily.	Data stored is Permanent.
We cannot establish relation between tables.	We can establish relation between tables.
Ex: Sysbase, Foxpro	Ex: Oracle, Sql Server

Question 58: What are ROLLUP and CUBE operators?

ROLLUP operator produces subtotal values and CUBE operator produces cross-tabulation values. Specify ROLLUP and CUBE operators in GROUP BY clause of a query.

Question 59: What is difference between Procedural and Non-Procedural language?

In procedural language you have to give complete set of instruction to perform a job whereas in Non-Procedural language you have to describe what to do rather than how to do a job.

Question 60: What is Normalization? Explain different types of normal forms?

Normalization is the process of efficiently organizing data in a database. It deals with elimination of redundant i.e. duplicate data and ensures data dependences i.e. only storing related data in a table. Therefore, Normalization helps in reducing the amount of space a database consumes and ensures data is logically stored.

Types of Normal forms:

a)   1NF: In 1NF repeating groups i.e. duplicate columns are eliminated. Separate tables are created for each group of related data and are identified by primary key.

b)   2NF: Table must be in 1NF. Partial dependency must be eliminated i.e. create primary-foreign key relationship.

c)   3NF: Table must be in 2NF. Remove columns that are not dependent upon primary key.

d)   4NF: Table must be in 3NF. A relation is in 4NF if it has no multi-valued dependencies.

e)   5NF: Relation should have only candidate keys and its primary key should consist of only single column.

Question 61: Why we use Normalization?

We use Normalization in order to show correct, accurate and reliable data.

Question 62: What are Pseudo columns?

Pseudo columns are not an actual column of any table but are used like a column of table. It cannot be modified or updated but are used only for retrieval purpose. It provides common information. For example: LEVEL, ROWID, ROWNUM, CURRVAL, NEXTVAL, SYSDATE, UID, USER etc.

Question 63: How to improve performance of SQL query?

Query Tuning can be done by following few points mentioned below:

a)   Create INDEX if the table is large or contains large number of NULL values.

b)   Do not create INDEX if the table is small or is updated frequently.

c)   Use the valid JOIN condition in the Query.

d)   Use TRUNCATE rather than DELETE statement, as TRUNCATE command releases the storage space.

e)   Use table alias with the column name if the query is complex.

f)   Do not use long column or table names.

g)   Create table containing related information.

h) Never mix data types

i) Create VIEWS for data safety

j) Use DECODE and CASE for complex queries as these functions can minimize the number of times a table has to be selected.

k) Use BETWEEN instead of IN operator.

Question 64: Explain Software Development Life Cycle (SDLC) in brief?

The System Development Life Cycle (SDLC) is the overall process of developing software using a series of defined steps. The steps include:

System Investigation: Understanding the problem.

System Analysis: Understanding the solution.

System design: Creating the logical and physical components.

System Implementation: Placing completed system into operation.

System maintenance and Review: Evaluating the implemented system.

Question 65: What is Data Modelling?

Data Modelling is a process of exploring what kind of data needs to be stored and then creating the structure accordingly. Data Modelling is a two step process: a) Exploration of real environment, b) Creation of data structure i.e. Extract relevant data from environment and organizing in a structure way in database. Data structure involves: List of relevant entities, List of relevant attributes, Finding out the relation between entities, Creation of tables to represent entities, and creation of keys to represent entities.

Question 66: What is Data Mining?

Data Mining is a process of extracting knowledge from large amount of data.

Question 67: What is a Cluster?

Cluster is a schema object that contains data from one or more tables that are having the same column name. Oracle database stores together all the rows from all the tables that share same cluster key. A cluster can contain a maximum of 32 tables and upto 16 cluster key columns can be specified.

Question 68: What is a DFD?

DFD stands for Data Flow Diagram. DFD shows the relationship among the various business processes within the organization.

Question 69: What is a Partitioning? How many types of partitioning are there in oracle?

Partitioning means splitting on larger table into small tables according to some criteria. Partitioning helps in improving query performance. Partitioning are of 4 types: Range Partitioning, Hash Partitioning, List Partitioning and Composite Partitioning.

Question 70: What are ACID properties?

ACID properties are a set of properties that guarantees the database transactions are processed reliably.

Atomicity: If one part of the transaction fails, the entire transaction fails and the database state is left unchanged.

Consistency: Ensure that any transaction will bring the database from one valid state to another i.e. Any data written to the database must be valid according to all defined rules.

Isolation: Ensure that if number of transactions executed serially i.e. one after the other then each transaction has to execute in total isolation.

Durability: Means once a transaction has been committed, it cannot be undone.

Question 71: What is a Materialized View?

Views evaluate the data in the tables underlying the view definition at the time the view is queried. It is a logical view of your tables, with no data stored anywhere else. The upside of a view is that it will always return the latest data to you. The downside of a view is that its performance depends on how good a select statement the view is based on. If the select statement used by the view joins many tables, or uses joins based on non-indexed columns, the view could perform poorly. Materialized views are similar to regular views, in that they are a logical view of your data (based on a select statement), however, the underlying query result set has been saved to a table. The upside of this is that when you query a materialized view, you are querying a table, which may also be indexed. In addition, because all the joins have been resolved at materialized view refresh time, you pay the price of the join once (or as often as you refresh your materialized view), rather than each time you select from the materialized view. In addition, with query rewrite enabled, Oracle can optimize a query that selects from the source of your materialized view in such a way that it instead reads from your materialized view. In situations where you create materialized views as forms of aggregate tables, or as copies of frequently executed queries, this can greatly speed up the response time of your end user application. The downside though is that the data you get back from the materialized view is only as up to date as the last time the materialized view has been refreshed. Materialized views can be set to refresh manually, on a set schedule, or based on the database detecting a change in data from one of the underlying tables. Materialized views can be incrementally updated by combining them with materialized view logs, which act as change data capture sources on the underlying tables. Materialized views are most often used in data warehousing / business intelligence applications where querying large fact tables with thousands of millions of rows would result in query response times that resulted in an unusable application.

Question 72: What is Global Temporary Table?

The data in a global temporary table is private, such that data inserted by a session can only be accessed by that session. The session-specific rows in a global temporary table can be preserved for the whole session, or just for the current transaction. The ON COMMIT DELETE ROWS clause indicates that the data should be deleted at the end of the transaction. In contrast, the ON COMMIT PRESERVE ROWS clause indicates that rows should be preserved until the end of the session.

Question 73: What is Correlated Subqueries?

Correlated Subqueries are used for row-by-row processing. Each subquery is executed once for every row of the outer query. Correlated Subquery is a way of reading every row in a table and comparing values in each row against related data. It is used whenever a subquery returns a different result for each candidate row considered by the main query.

Question 74: What is difference between IN and EXISTS in SQL?

EXISTS clause is used for testing whether a given set is empty or not , returns the Boolean value either True or False. Whereas IN Clause is use to check every values that exists in the given set to the corresponding condition. EXISTS condition is faster than IN condition in case the condition needs to test for the existence of values in the set.

Question 75: What is difference between Bitmap and B-Tree Indexes?

Bitmap Indexes are most effective for queries that contain multiple conditions in the where clause. Bitmap indexes are primarily intended for data warehousing applications where users query the data rather than performing DML operations. B-Tree Indexes are the default indexes and is used when you know that your query refers the indexed column and will retrieves only few rows.

Question 76: What is a difference between Views and Materialized Views?

Views	Materialized View (MV)
View store Select statement of a query	Store result-set of a query

Refreshed automatically	Need to refresh externally
Need to call a query by using view name	When querying the table, Materialized Views used automatically.
Slower as compared to MV when querying larger table	Faster
Cannot create index on Views.	Can create index on MV

Question 77: What is an EXPLAIN PLAN Statement?

The EXPLAIN PLAN checks the feasibility of a query. The EXPLAIN PLAN statement allows you to submit a SQL statement to Oracle and have the database prepare the execution plan for the statement without actually executing it. The execution plan is made available to you in the form of rows inserted into a special table called a plan table. You may query the rows in the plan table using ordinary SELECT statements in order to see the steps of the execution plan for the statement you explained. EXPLAIN PLAN is handy for evaluating individual SQL statements. The PLAN table includes columns like operations, object name, number of rows affected, size, cost etc.

Question 78: What is a TKPROF Utility?

TKPROF is a utility that you invoke at the operating system level in order to analyze SQL trace files and generate reports that present the trace information in a readable form. SQL trace files are text files that, strictly speaking, are human readable. In other words, you can say that TKPROF is a program that you invoke at the operating system command prompt in order to reformat the trace file into a format that is much easier to comprehend.

Question 79: Define three models of Design Phase in SCDL?

The three models of design phase in SCDL are:

1) Conceptual Data Model: It considers the business processes and rules that applied to the relevant information. It deals with how stored data is going to be used irrelevant to how information is stored and managed. It is applied to both application and data design.

2) Logical Data Model: Normalization concepts come into this stage. Data structure is defined or analyzed.

3) Physical Data Model: Finally, the data structure is created here.

Question 80: Explain few steps for Performance Tuning?

Performance Tuning on SQL and PL/SQL can be performed by following few guidelines:

1) Database must be normalized which will help to decrease the storage requirement and faster search performance.

2) Use proper join conditions on complex queries.

3) Create indexes properly when and where required.

4) Use Order by clause for an index scan.

5) Use Exists clause instead of IN operator.

6) Use views when few columns need to be selected from multiple tables.

7) Use materialized views when performing complex calculations on larger tables.

8) Use SQL Hints for performance.

9) Use EXPLAIN PLAN and TKPROF for getting the execution plan of the statements.

10) Use BULK COLLECT and FORALL statements to reduce context switch between SQL and PL/SQL engine.

Best 60 PL/SQL Questions and Answers

Question 1: Describe in brief about PL/SQL?

PL/SQL is a procedural extension to SQL with design features of programming language such as Data encapsulation, Information hiding, Exception handling etc. Oracle Server and oracle tools (oracle developer) have their own PL/SQL engine. PL/SQL Engine processes the entire PL/SQL block and filters out the SQL and procedural Statements separately, this reduces the amount of work that is sent to the oracle server and the number of memory cursors that are required. SQL data types can also be used in PL/SQL. PL/SQL code can be stored in oracle server as subprograms and can be referenced by any number of applications that are connected to the database.

Question 2: What are the benefits of using PL/SQL?

Few benefits of using PL/SQL are:

a)   PL/SQL improves performance and reduces network traffic by sending the entire block to the Oracle server in a single transfer.

b)   PL/SQL block can be nested.

c)   PL/SQL code is reusable.

d)   PL/SQL is portable, can run on any platform where oracle server can run.

e)   Can declare Variables

f)   Can control the flow of execution of statements through control statements i.e. IF statement Case statement, Loop controls structures.

g)   Allow multi-row processing through explicit cursors.

h)   PL/SQL can handle errors.

i)   PL/SQL code is easy to maintain.

j)   PL/SQL improved data security and Integrity (related actions are performed together).

Question 3: What are the sections described in PL/SQL block?

PL/SQL block consists of 3 sections:

a) Declarative Section (optional): Can declare Variables, Constants, Cursors and User-defined exceptions

b) Executable Section (mandatory): Contains SQL and PL/SQL Statements.

c) Exception Handling Section (optional): Actions to perform when errors occurs.

Question 4: Describe the types of PL/SQL block?

There are 2 different types of PL/SQL block:

1)   Anonymous Blocks: Are unnamed block that does not accept parameters.

2)   Subprograms: Are named PL/SQL block that can accept parameters and can be invoked. Subprograms are of two types:

a)   Procedures: Used to perform an action.

b)   Function: Used to compute a value. A function is similar to procedure except that a function must return a value.

Question 5: What is a PL/SQL variable?

PL/SQL Variable can be used for temporary storage of data, reusability and manipulation of stored values.

Question 6: Describe %Type in PL/SQL?

%Type is used to declare variable based on the definition of database column. If the definition changes, the variable declaration changes accordingly at runtime.

Question 7: What are different types of Modes used in PL/SQL parameter?

Values into the PL/SQL Subprograms can be passed through parameters by using three modes IN, OUT and INOUT modes.

a) IN Mode: Used to pass values to the subprogram being called. It is a default type. Can be assigned a default value.

b) OUT Mode: Used to return values to the caller of a subprogram. Cannot assigned a default value.

c) INOUT Mode: Used to pass initial values to the subprogram being called and return an updated value to the caller of the subprograms. It cannot be assigned a default value.

Question 8: What are the data type categories supported by PL/SQL variables?

PL/SQL Variables supports four different data type categories:-

a)   Scalar Data Types: Used to hold single value.

b)   Composite Data Types: Used to hold group of fields called records.

c)   Reference Data Types: Used to hold values called Pointers that refer to other program items.

d)   LOB (Large Objects) Data Types: Used to hold values called Locators that specify the location of large objects such as Graphics Images, Videos, and Photos etc.

Question 9: What is a Host or Bind variable?

Host and Bind variables are non-PL/SQL variables. Are used to pass run-time values out of the PL/SQL block back to the iSQL*Plus Environment. These variables are referred in a PL/SQL block with a preceding colon.

Question 10: What is PRINT and VARIABLE commands?

PRINT and VARIABLE are iSQL*Plus commands. Use VARIABLE command to declare bind variable and use PRINT command to display current value of bind variables.

Question 11: What is the use of DEFINE_OUTPUT.PUT_LINE command?

It is an Oracle-supplied packaged procedure, an alternative of PRINT command for displaying data from a PL/SQL block. It must be enabled with SET SERVEROUTPUT ON.

Question 12: What are Identifiers?

Identifiers are used to name PL/SQL program items and units which include constants, variables, Exceptions, cursor variables, subprograms and packages. Identifiers can contains up to 30 characters, must begin with an alphabetic character. Can contains numerals, dollar signs, underscores and number signs but cannot contain characters such as hyphens, slashes and spaces and should not be a reserved words.

Question 13: What is a CHR function?

CHR Function is the SQL function that converts ASCII code to its corresponding character. For example: 10 is the code for a line feed.

V_add:=v_name|CHR(10)||V_address||CHR(10)||V_zip;

Question 14: Describe loop control structure in PL/SQL?

Loop control structure controls the flow of execution of the PL/SQL statements. Loop Control Structures are of three types:

a) BASIC Loop: Allows the execution of its statement at least once even if the condition is already met upon entering the loop. Without the EXIT statement the loop would be infinite. A BASIC loop can contain multiple EXIT statements. EXIT Statement is used to terminate a loop. Control passes to the next statement after the END LOOP statement.

b) WHILE Loop: Is used to repeat a sequence of statements based on some condition. Condition is evaluated at the start of each iteration.

c) FOR Loop: Is used if the number of iterations is known .i.e. how many times you want to execute the loop.

Question 15: Describe %RowType in PL/SQL?

%RowType is used to declare a variable of record data type that is based on the definition of database Table. If the definition changes the variable declaration also changes accordingly at runtime.

Question 16: What are Cursors?

Cursors are private SQL areas defined by the Oracle Server to execute the SQL Statements and to store the processing information. Cursors are of two types: Implicit Cursors and Explicit Cursors.

Question 17: What is a difference between Implicit and Explicit cursors?

The main difference between Implicit and Explicit cursors is:

Implicit Cursors	Explicit Cursors
Are declared by PL/SQL implicitly for queries that return only one row.	Are declared and named by the programmer for queries that return more than one row.

Are less efficient than explicit cursors as it is harder to trap data errors.	Can easily trap data errors
The user is unaware of this and cannot control or process the information in an implicit cursor.	The explicit cursor gives the programmer more programmatic control.
Cursor attributes are : SQL%ROWCOUNT, SQL%FOUND, SQL%NOTFOUND and SQL%ISOPEN	Cursor attributes are : %ROWCOUNT, %FOUND, %NOTFOUND and %ISOPEN
Oracle server implicitly opens and closes the cursor.	The PL/SQL program opens a cursor, processes rows returned by a query and then closes the cursor. The cursor makes the current position in the Active set.

Question 18: What is an Active set?

The set of rows returned by a multiple-row query is called Active set.

Question 19: What is the difference between FOR UPDATE CLAUSE and NO WAIT?

FOR UPDATE CLAUSE: Is used to lock record while updating or deleting record so that no another user can changed that record before you complete the transaction.

NO WAIT: Is used to tell oracle server not to wait if requested rows have been locked by another User. Control is immediately returned to your program so that it can do another work before trying again to acquire the lock. If you omit the NO WAIT keyword, oracle waits until the rows are available.

Question 20: Describe WHERE CURRENT OF clause?

WHERE CURRENT OF clause is used to reference the current row from an explicit cursor. It is used with FOR UPDATE clause but cannot be used with LOCK TABLE statement.

Question 21: What is an Exception? Describe different types of exceptions in PL/SQL?

Exception is an identifier in PL/SQL that is raised during execution. Exception can be raised by two means: When an oracle error occurs and when you raise it explicitly. A block always terminates when PL/SQL raises an exception.

Exception can be of three types:

a)   Predefined Oracle Server: do not declare, Implicitly raised

b) Non-predefined Oracle Server: Declare explicitly, implicitly raised

c) User-Defined: Declare and raise explicitly.

Question 22: What are the two functions used for trapping Exceptions?

SQLCODE and SQLERRM are the two functions for trapping exceptions. SQLCODE returns the numeric value for the error code, while, SQLERRM returns the message associated with the error number.

Question 23: What is a difference between Procedure and Function?

The main difference between Procedure and Function is:

Procedure	Function
Is used to perform an action	Is used to compute a value
Execute as a PL/SQL statement	Invoke as a part of an expression.
Do not contain RETURN clause in the header section	Must contain a RETURN clause in the Header section.
Can return none, one or many values.	Must return a single value.
Can contain a RETURN statement	Must contain at least one RETURN statement.

Question 24: What is difference between Formal and Actual Parameters?

The main difference between Formal and Actual Parameters is as below:

Formal parameters are those parameters where variables are declared in the parameter list of the subprogram specification.

For example: Create procedure raise_sal (p_id number, p_amt number)......

Here, P_id and P_amt are the formal parameters.

Actual Parameters are those parameters where variables or expressions are referenced in the parameter list of a subprogram Call.

For example: Raise_sal (v_id,2000).

Here, V_id and 2000 are the Actual parameters.

Question 25: What are the different methods of passing values to the parameters?

There are three different methods of passing values to the parameters:

a) **Positional:** List Actual parameters in the same order as formal parameters.

b) **Named:** List Actual parameters in arbitrary order by associating each one with its formal parameter name, using special syntax. (=>)

c) **Combination:** List the first value positionally and the remainder using the special syntax of the named method.

Question 26: What are the restrictions for calling a Function from an expression?

To be callable from SQL expressions, a user-defined function must:

a) Be a stored function.

b) Accept only IN Parameter mode.

c) Accept only valid SQL data types, not PL/SQL specific types, as parameters.

d) Return data type that is valid SQL data types, not PL/SQL specific types.

e) Functions called from SQL expressions cannot contain DML statements.

f) Functions called from an UPDATE/DELETE statement on a table 'T' cannot query (select) or contain DML on the same table 'T'.

g) Functions called from SQL statements cannot contain statements that end the transactions.

Question 27: What is difference between AUTHID CURRENT USER and AUTHID DEFINER?

AUTHID CURRENT USER is use to ensure that the procedure executes using the security of the executing user and not the owner. AUTHID DEFINER is used to ensure that the procedure executes using the owner's privileges.

Question 28: What is different between USER_OBJECTS, USER_SOURCE and USER_ERRORS data dictionary tables?

USER_OBJECTS stores the object (Table, Procedure, Function, package, Package Body, trigger) information. USER_SOURCE stores the source code (text of the objects) and USER_ERRORS stores the text for compile errors, (PL/SQL syntax errors).

Question 29: What is a DBMS_OUTPUT?

DBMS_OUTPUT stores the run-time debug information. It accumulates information into a buffer and allows retrieval of the information from the buffer.

Question 30: What are Packages in PL/SQL?

Package group logically related PL/SQL types, items and subprograms. Package cannot be invoked, parameterized or nested. Package allows the oracle server to load multiple objects into memory at once, thus later calls to constructs in the same package requires no disk I/O. Package consists of two parts:

a) Package Specification: Contains Public Constructs. It is accessible to the outside environment.

b) Package Body: Contains Private Constructs. It is hidden and inaccessible to the outside environment.

Package specification and body are stored separately in the database but must have the same name.

Question 31: What are the advantages of using Package?

Some of the advantages of using Package are:

a)   **Modularity:** Encapsulate related constructs.

b)   **Easier Application Design:** Code and compile specification and body separately.

c)   **Hiding Information:** Private constructs in the package body are hidden and inaccessible. All coding is hidden in the package Body.

d)   **Better performance:** There is only one copy in memory for all users. The entire package is loaded into memory when the package is first referenced; no further disk I/O is required.

e)   **Overloading:** Multiple subprograms of the same name.

Question 32: What is Overloading in PL/SQL?

Overloading enables you to use the same name for different subprograms inside a PL/SQL block, a subprogram or a Package. Require the formal parameter of the subprograms to differ in number, order or data type family. Most built-in functions are overloaded. For ex: TO_CHAR function of standard package.

Question 33: What do you mean by Forward Declaration in a Package?

Forward Declarations means a program must be declared before calling it. Forward declaration is used to do the following:

a)   Define subprogram in logical or alphabetical order.

b)   Define mutually recursive subprograms.

c)   Group subprograms in a package.

Question 34: What do you mean by One-Time only procedure in a Package?

One-Time only procedure is executed only once, when the package is first invoked within the user session. The keyword END is not used at the end of a one-time only.

Question 35: What are Triggers in PL/SQL?

Trigger is a PL/SQL block or a PL/SQL Procedure associated with a table, view, schema or the database. Trigger is executed implicitly whenever a particular event takes place. Design Triggers to perform related actions and to centralize global operations. Database triggers fire for every user each time the event occurs for which the Trigger is created.

Question 36: Describe components of Trigger?

Three components of Trigger are:

a) Trigger Timing: When the Trigger fires in relation to the Triggering event. (possible values are:- BEFORE, AFTER, INSTEAD OF)

b) Triggering Event: Which data manipulation operation on the table or view causes the Trigger to fire. (Possible values are: INSERT, UPDATE and DELETE).

c) Trigger Type: How many times the Trigger body executes. (Possible values are: STATEMENT, ROW).

Question 37: What is difference between BEFORE, AFTER and INSTEAD OF Trigger?

Before Trigger is used to determine whether the Triggering statement should be allowed to complete. **After Trigger** is used to complete the triggering statement before executing the Triggering action and **Instead of Trigger** are used for views which cannot be modified directly.

Question 38: What is a difference between STATEMENT and ROW Trigger?

Statement Trigger: This is the default. A statement Trigger is fired once on behalf of the triggering event, even if no rows are affected. **Row trigger:** Fired for each row affected by the Triggering event. If the triggering event affects no rows, a row trigger is not executed.

Question 39: What is a difference between database Trigger and stored Procedure?

The main difference between database Trigger and stored Procedure is:

Triggers	Procedures
Defines with CREATE TRIGGER syntax	Defines with CREATE PROCEDURE syntax
Data dictionary contains source code in USER_TRIGGERS	Data dictionary contains source code in USER_SOURCE
Implicitly Invoked	Explicitly Invoked
Commit, Savepoint and Rollback are not allowed.	Commit, Savepoint and Rollback are allowed.

Question 40: What is the use of DBMS_PIPE?

DBMS_PIPE enables messages to send between sessions.

Question 41: What do you mean by Dependent and Referenced objects in PL/SQL?

Some Objects reference other objects as part of their definition. For ex: Stored Procedure could contain a SELECT statement that selects columns from a table. For this reason, the stored procedure is called a Dependent object, whereas the table is called a Reference Object.

Question 42: What is Dynamic SQL? Explain in brief?

Dynamic SQL is a SQL statement that contains variables that can change during runtime. Dynamic SQL is written using either DBMS_SQL or native dynamic SQL Execute Immediate.

EXECUTE IMMEDIATE: The Execute Immediate statement can perform dynamic single-row queries. Also, this is used for functionality such as objects and collections, which are not supported by DBMS_SQL.

DBMS_SQL: The DBMS_SQL is used to perform dynamically multi-row query. DBMS_SQL package is used to write dynamic SQL in stored procedures and to parse DDL statements. Some of the procedures and functions of the package include:

a)   OPEN_CURSOR: Opens a new cursor and assigns a cursor ID number.

b)   PARSE: Every SQL statement must be parsed. Parsing the statement includes checking the statements syntax and validating the statement, ensuring that all references to objects are correct and ensuring that the relevant privileges to those objects exist.

c)   BIND_VARIABLES: Binds the given value to the variable identified by its name in the parsed statement in the given cursor.

d)   EXECUTE: Executes the SQL statement and returns the number of row processed.

e)   FETCH_ROWS: Retrieves a row for the specified cursor (for multiple rows, call in a loop)

f)   CLOSE_CURSOR: Closes the specified cursor.

Question 43: Describe the use of LOB data type?

LOB is a data type that is used to store large, unstructured data such as text, graphics, images, Video clipping and so on.

There are four types of LOB'S:

a)   BLOB: Represents Binary large objects, such as Video clips.

b)   CLOB: Represents a character large object.

c)   NCLOB: Represents a multi byte character large object

d)   BFILE: Represents a binary file. The BFILE column or attributes stores a file locator that points to the external file.

Question 44: What is a difference between LONG and LOB data types?

The main difference between LONG and LOB data types is:

LONG AND LONG RAW	LOB
Single LONG column per table	Multiple LOB column per table
Size up to 2GB	Size up to 4GB
SELECT returns data	SELECT returns Locator.
Data stored in-line	Data stored in-line or out-of-line
Sequential access to data	Random access to data

Question 45: Name the utility to trace in which line the error was raised in PL/SQL?

DBMS_UTILITY.FORMAT_ERROR_BACKTRACE ( )

Question 46: What is Autonomous Transaction?

Autonomous Transaction is independent of the main transaction. You cannot exit the active autonomous transaction without commit and rollback. Autonomous transaction is declared with pragma. For example:

Create or Replace Procedure Autonomous_Proc As

Pragma autonomous_transaction;

[PL/SQL block]....

Question 47: What is Collection? How many types of collection are there?

Collection is a group of elements of same data type. Collections are used just like ordinary data type and they can be passed as parameter. Collections are of two types: Tables and Varray.

Question 48: What is a difference between Varray and Nested Table?

The main difference between Varray and Nested Table are:

1) There is a fixed upper bound in case of Varray, whereas in Nested Table there is no upper bound i.e. you can store unlimited values in Nested Table.

2) Varray are dense and Nested Tables are sparse i.e. you cannot delete an individual element from Varray.
3) LIMIT method when used with Nested table returns NULL as Nested table do not have a maximum size.

Question 49: What is a PRAGMA?

PRAGMA is also called Pseudo instructions. PRAGMA is a special instruction to the PL/SQL compiler. PRAGMA is the keyword that signifies that the statement is a compiler directive, which is not processed when the PL/SQL block is executed. It is important to note that pragmas are processed at the time of the compilation.

Question 50: What are Records? Explain different types of Records with example?

Record is similar to a row of a database table. Records are of three types:

a)   Table Based: Is used to define a variable based on the definition of database table. For example:

Emp_rec emp%rowtype

b)   Cursor Based: Is used to define a variable based on the definition of user defined cursor.

For example:

     Cursor C1 is select * from employee;

Emp_rec C1%rowtype

c)   User-Defined Records: Is used to create data type of record type. For example:

Type Emp_Rec_Type is Record (empno number, empname Varchar2(20));

Emp_Rec Emp_Rec_Type

Declared a variable "Emp_Rec" of datatype "Emp_Rec_Type"

Question 51: What is a NOCOPY hint in PL/SQL?

NOCOPY is used typically with OUT and INOUT parameters. By default OUT and INOUT parameters are passed by value. This means that the values of the parameter are copied before the subprogram or method is executed. Than during execution temporary variables are used to hold values of the OUT parameter. By adding a NOCOPY hint, you instruct the PL/SQL compiler to pass OUT and INOUT parameter by reference and eliminate the copying step.

Question 52: What is a difference between Nested Tables and Associative Arrays (Index by Table)?

The main difference between these two types is:

1) Nested table can be stored in a database column, where as Associative Arrays cannot.
2) Nested table must be initialized before its individual elements can be referenced i.e. It must be initialized with the help of a system-defined function called a constructor. The constructor has the same name as the nested table type whereas, Associative array do not requires to get initialized.
3) EXTEND method cannot be used with Associative array.
4) TRIM method cannot be used with index-by tables.

Question 53: What are the various Collection methods?

The various Collection methods are:

1) EXISTS: EXISTS(n) returns TRUE if the nth element in a collection exists. Otherwise, EXISTS(n) returns FALSE
2) COUNT: Returns the number of elements that a collection currently contains.
3) EXTEND: used to increase the size of a collection.
4) DELETE: This procedure has three forms. DELETE removes all elements from a collection. DELETE (n) removes the nth element from an associative array or nested table. If n is null, DELETE (n) does nothing. DELETE (m, n) removes all elements in the range m...n from an associative array or nested table. If m is larger than n or if m or n is null, DELETE (m, n) does nothing.
5) FIRST and LAST: FIRST and LAST return the first and last (smallest and largest) subscript values in a collection
6) PRIOR and NEXT: PRIOR (n) returns the subscript that precedes index n in a collection. NEXT (n) returns the subscript that succeeds index n. If n has no predecessor, PRIOR (n) returns NULL. Likewise, if n has no successor, NEXT (n) returns NULL.
7) TRIM: removes one element from the end of a collection. TRIM(n) removes n elements from the end of a collection.

Question 54: What is a Context switch in PLSQL?

PL/SQL engine sends SQL statements to the SQL engine, which returns results to the PL/SQL engine. The communication between the PL/SQL and SQL engines is called a Context switch.

Question 55: What is a BULK SQL?

A certain amount of performance overhead is associated with the context switches. However, the PL/SQL language has a number of features that can minimize the performance overhead known as Bulk SQL. Generally, if a SQL statement affects four or more rows, bulk SQL many improve performance significantly. Bulk SQL supports batch processing of SQL statements and their results. It consists of two features: - the FORALL statement and the BULK COLLECT clause. The FORALL statements sends INSERT, UPDATE or DELETE statements in batches from PL/SQL to SQL instead of one at a time. The BULK COLLECT is use to fetch or select all rows in a single go rather than one at a time.

Question 56: What is the difference between Rule based Optimizer and Cost based Optimizer in oracle?

Rule based Optimizer (RBO): In brief the rule-based method means that when executing a query the database must follow certain predefined rules and matter what data is stored in affected database tables.

A long time ago the only optimizer in the Oracle database was the Rule-Based Optimizer (RBO). Basically the RBO used a set of rules to determine how to execute a query. If an index was available on a table the RBO rules said to always use the index. There are some cases where the use of an index slowed down a query. For example assume someone put an index on the GENDER column which holds one of two values MALE and FEMALE.

Then someone issues the following query:

SELECT * FROM emp WHERE gender 'FEMALE';

If the above query returned approximately 50 of the rows then using an index would actually slow things down. It would be faster to read the entire table and throw away all rows that have MALE values. Experts in Oracle query optimization have come to a rule of thumb that says if the number of rows returned is more than 5-10 of the total table volume using an index would slow things down. The RBO would always use an index if present because its rules said to.

It became obvious that the RBO armed with its set of discrete rules did not always make great decisions. The biggest problem with the RBO was that it did not take the data distribution into account. So the Cost-Based Optimizer (CBO) was born. The CBO uses statistics about the table its indexes and the data distribution to make better informed decisions.

Using our previous example assume that the company has employees that are 95 female and 5 male. If you query for females then you do not want to use the index. If you query for males then you would like to use the index. The CBO has information at hand to help make these kinds of determinations that were not available in the old RBO.

Cost based Optimizer (CBO): The Oracle cost-based optimizer is designed to determine the most efficient way to carry out a SQL statement. In cost-based method the database must decide which query execution plan to choose using best guess approach that takes into account what data is stored in db.

Question 57: What are the advantages of using Triggers in PL/SQL?

The main advantages of using Triggers are:

1) Enforces complex business rules that cannot be defined using integrity constraints.
2) Maintaining complex security rules
3) Preventing invalid transactions.
4) Providing value auditing
5) Perform related actions and centralize global operations
6) Collecting statistical information on table accesses.

Question 58: What are REF Cursors? Give one example?

A REF Cursor is a datatype that holds a cursor value in the same way that a VARCHAR2 variable will hold a string value. REF Cursors are used to associate query at runtime.

For Example:

Create a function that opens a cursor and returns a reference to it:

```
CREATE OR REPLACE FUNCTION f RETURN SYS_REFCURSOR
AS
  c SYS_REFCURSOR;
BEGIN
  OPEN c FOR select * from dual;
  RETURN c;
END;
/
```

Call the above function and fetch all rows from the cursor it returns:

```
Set serveroutput on
DECLARE
  c SYS_REFCURSOR;
  v VARCHAR2(1);
BEGIN
  c := f();  -- Get ref cursor from function
  LOOP
    FETCH c into v;
    EXIT WHEN c%NOTFOUND;
    dbms_output.put_line('Value from cursor: '||v);
  END LOOP;
END;
/
```

Question 59: Explain UTL_FILE in detail?

With the UTL_FILE package, PL/SQL programs can read and write operating system text files. UTL_FILE provides a restricted version of operating system stream file I/O.

Subprograms in UTL_FILE:

1) FILE_TYPE: The datatype for a file handle
2) IS_OPEN: This function has a return datatype of BOOLEAN. It returns true if the file is open and false if the file is closed.
3) FOPEN: Opens a file for input or output. The mode to open a file is R: Read, W: Write and A: Append.
4) FCLOSE: Closes a file.
5) FCLOSE_ALL: Closes all open file handles.
6) FFLUSH: Physically writes all pending output to a file.
7) GET_LINE: Reads text from an open file
8) PUT_LINE: Writes a line to a file
9) NEW_LINE: Inserts a new line terminator into the opened text file.
10) PUTF: This procedure puts formatted text into the opened file.

Question 60: What is a PRAGMA Exception_Init in Exception handling?

It tells the compiler to associate an exception name with an oracle error number.

Best 51 Solved Basic SQL Queries

1) SQL query to create partition by range on a table

    create table product (**product_id** number, **product_name** varchar2(30),
    Manufactured_Date date)
    partition by range (**Manufactured_Date**)
    (
    partition **part1** values less than (TO_DATE('2013-01-01 00:00:00', 'YYYY-MM-DD
    HH24:MI:SS')),
    partition **part2** values less than (TO_DATE('2014-01-01 00:00:00', 'YYYY-MM-DD
    HH24:MI:SS'))
    );

2) SQL query to create database link

    CREATE DATABASE LINK <DATABASE_LINK_NAME>
    CONNECT TO <SCHEMA_NAME>
    IDENTIFIED BY <PWD>
    USING <DATABASE_NAME>;

3) SQL query to create comments on a table

    Comment on table temp is 'This is a Test Table';

    [Where "temp" is a table]

4) SQL query to create comments on a table column

    Comment on column temp.**user_name** is 'This is a Test User'

    [Where "temp" is a table name and "user_name" is a column]

5) SQL query to create bitmap index on a table

    Create bitmap index **idx_gender** on employee (**gender**);

    [Where "idx_gender" is an Index name]

6) SQL query to create function-based index on a table

    create index **idx_empname_upper** on employee (upper(**empname**));

[Where "idx_empname_upper" is an Index name]

7) SQL query to disable and enable constraints on a table

Alter table employee disable constraint <constraint_name>;

Alter table employee enable constraint <constraint_name>;

8) SQL query to add foreign key constraint on a table

Alter table employee add constraint emp_mgr_fk foreign key (manager_id) references employee (employee_id);

[Where "emp_mgr_fk" is a constraint name]

9) SQL query to drop constraint from a table

Alter table employee drop constraint <constraint_name>;

10) SQL query to rename table name

Rename employee to employee_new;

[Where"employee" is old table name and "employee_new" is a new table name]

11) SQL query to rename column name

Alter table employee rename column empname to emp_name;

[Where"empname" is old column name and "emp_name" is a new column name]

12) SQL query to make table read only

Alter table employee read only;

Write below query to make table read and write.

Alter table employee read write;

13) SQL query to copy structure of a table

Create table employee_new as select * from employee where 1>2;

[Where"employee_new" is a copied table to "employee" table without any data]

14) SQL query using MERGE statement

```
MERGE INTO bonuses D
USING (SELECT employee_id, salary, department_id FROM employees
WHERE department_id = 80) S
ON (D.employee_id = S.employee_id)
WHEN MATCHED THEN UPDATE SET D.bonus = D.bonus + S.salary*.01
DELETE WHERE (S.salary > 8000)
WHEN NOT MATCHED THEN INSERT (D.employee_id, D.bonus)
VALUES (S.employee_id, S.salary*.01)
WHERE (S.salary <= 8000);
```

15) SQL query using LIKE condition

Select * from employee where emp_name like 'Sh%';

[Above query will display all employees whose name started with letter "Sh"]

16) SQL query to make a string case-sensitive.

Select upper ('john') from dual // All characters in upper case

Output: JOHN

Select lower ('JOHN') from dual // All characters in lower case

Output: john

Select initcap ('joHn') from dual //first character in upper case

Output: John

17) SQL query to calculate the length of a string value

Select length ('john') from dual

Length of "john" is: 4

18) SQL query to pad blank space up to a maximum length

select lpad ('TESTING',10,'*') from dual; //Left Padding

Output: ***TESTING

select rpad ('TESTING',10,'*') from dual; // Right Padding

Output: TESTING***

[Here 10 is the maximum length for padding]

19) SQL query to return remainder of a division

Select mod (1500, 200) from dual;

Output: 100   [Remainder is 1500/200 = 100]

20) SQL query to find number of weeks fall between two dates

[Suppose Start Date is '01-Nov-2014' and End Date is "30-Nov-2014"]

Select (to_date ('30-Nov-2014','DD-MON-YYYY') - to_date('01-Nov-2014','DD-MON-YYYY'))/7 from dual;

Output: 4.14 weeks

21) SQL query to find last day of a month

[Suppose Start Date is '01-Nov-2014']

Select last_day (to_date('01-Nov-2014','DD-MON-YYYY')) from dual;

Output: 30-Nov-2014

22) SQL query to find next day of a month

[Suppose Start Date is '01-Nov-2014' and is a Saturday]

Select next_day (to_date('01-Nov-2014','DD-MON-YYYY'),'friday') from dual;

Output: 07-Nov-2014 [Next Friday will be on 07-Nov-2014]

23) SQL query to find number of months between two dates

[Suppose Start Date is '01-Jul-2014' and End Date is "30-Nov-2014"]

Select months_between(to_date ('30-Nov-2014','DD-MON-YYYY') , to_date('01-Jul-2014','DD-MON-YYYY'))from dual;

Output: 4.94

24) SQL query to add number of months to a date

Select add_months (to_date('01-Nov-2014','DD-MON-YYYY'),2) from dual;

Output: 01-Jan-2015

25) SQL query to get the first day of a month

Select trunc(to_date('30-Nov-2014','DD-MON-YYYY'),'month')from dual;

Output: 01-Nov-2014

26) SQL query to get the first day of a Year

Select trunc(to_date('30-Nov-2014','DD-MON-YYYY'),'Year')from dual;

Output: 01-Jan-2014

27) SQL query to spell a day

Select To_char(to_date('20-Nov-2014','DD-MON-YYYY'),'ddspth')from dual;

Output: twentieth [day 20 is spelled as twentieth]

28) SQL query to replace null value with another value

Select nvl ('','Testing Null Values') from dual;

Output: Testing Null Values

29) SQL query using CASE and DECODE function

[Create one test table "Suppliers" and add few rows into it as below]

Create table suppliers (supplier_id number, supplier_name varchar2(100));

```
Insert into suppliers values (10000, 'ABC');
Insert into suppliers values (10001, 'XYZ');
Insert into suppliers values (10002, 'LMN');
Commit;
```

CASE Statement:

```
SELECT supplier_name,
CASE
```

```
when supplier_id=10000 THEN 'IBM'
when supplier_id=10001 THEN 'Microsoft'
when supplier_id=10002 THEN 'Hewlett Packard'
ELSE NULL end result
FROM suppliers;
```

(OR)

```
SELECT supplier_name,
CASE
supplier_id when 10000 THEN 'IBM'
when 10001 THEN 'Microsoft'
when 10002 THEN 'Hewlett Packard'
ELSE NULL end result
FROM suppliers;
```

Output:

SUPPLIER_NAME	RESULT
ABC	IBM
XYZ	Microsoft
LMN	Hewlett Packard

DECODE Function:

```
SELECT supplier_name,
DECODE (supplier_id, 10000, 'IBM',
        10001, 'Microsoft',
        10002, 'Hewlett Packard',
        'Gateway') result
FROM suppliers;
```

Output:

SUPPLIER_NAME	RESULT
ABC	IBM
XYZ	Microsoft
LMN	Hewlett Packard

30) SQL query to create inline view

```
SELECT * FROM
(SELECT deptno, count (*) emp_count FROM emp GROUP BY deptno) emp,
```

```
//is a Inline View
dept
WHERE dept.deptno = emp.deptno
```

31)SQL query to find top three earnings employees

[Create one test table "emp" and add few rows into it as below]

create table emp (eno number, ename varchar2(30),esal number);

insert into emp values (101,'Sachin',50000);
insert into emp values (102,'Anil',20000);
insert into emp values (103,'Naveen',30000);
insert into emp values (104,'Naman',20000);
insert into emp values (105,'John',40000);
insert into emp values (106,'Peter',45000);
commit;

select ename,esal,rownum as "RANK" from (select ename,esal from emp order by esal desc) where rownum<=3;

Output:

ENAME	ESAL	RANK
Sachin	50000	1
Peter	45000	2
John	40000	3

32)SQL query to create sequence range from 100 to 10,000 and increment by 15

```
CREATE SEQUENCE SEQ_TEST
START WITH 100
INCREMENT BY 15
MAXVALUE 10000
MINVALUE 1
NOCYCLE
CACHE 20
NOORDER;
```

33)SQL query to get current and next available sequence number

Select SEQ_TEST.nextval from dual; //get next available number

Select SEQ_TEST.currval from dual; // get current available number

34) SQL query to create synonym for a table name.

Create synonym emp for employee;

[where "emp" is a synonym to "employee" table name]

35) SQL query to create and change password of a user

Create user <user_name> identified by <pass_word>; // Create User

Alter user <user_name> identified by <pass_word>; // Change Password

36) SQL query to grant system privileges to a user

Grant create session, create table, create sequence, create view to <user_name>;

37) SQL query to create a role and grant it to a user

Create role <role_name>; //Create Role

Grant create table, create view to <role_name>; // Grant privileges to role

Grant <role_name> to <user_name1>, <user_name2>; // Grant Role to Users

38) SQL query to revoke select and insert privileges from a user

Revoke select, insert on <table_name> from <user_name>;

39) SQL query to display all data from Table 1 that is missing in Table 2

[Where, Table 1 and Table 2 are having same column name]

Select * from <Table1>
Minus
Select * from <Table2>;

40) SQL query to get all distinct data from table 1 and table 2

[Where, Table 1 and Table 2 are having same column name]

Select * from <Table1>
Union
Select * from <Table2>;

41) SQL query to display all data from table 1 and table 2

[Where, Table 1 and Table 2 are having same column name]

```
Select * from <Table1>
Union All
Select * from <Table2>;
```

42)SQL query to get number of records in a table

```
Select count (*) from employee;
```

(OR)

```
Select count (1) from employee;
```

43)SQL query to get sub-total values from a table

[Create one test table "emp" and add few rows into it as below]

```
Create table emp (eno number,deptid number,jobtype varchar2(30),salary number)

Insert into emp values (101,10,'Assistant', 10000);
Insert into emp values (102,20,'Analyst', 50000);
Insert into emp values (103,20,'Clerk', 12000);
Insert into emp values (104,30,'Assistant', 20000);
Insert into emp values (105,30,'Manager', 60000);
Insert into emp values (106,30,'Sr analyst', 55000);
Insert into emp values (107,40,'Team Lead', 44000);
Commit;
```

```
select deptid,jobtype,sum(salary) from emp group by rollup (deptid,jobtype) order
by deptid;
```

Output:

DEPTID	JOBTYPE	SUM(SALARY)
10	Assistant	10000
10		10000
20	Analyst	50000
20	Clerk	12000
20		62000
30	Assistant	20000
30	Manager	60000
30	Sr analyst	55000

30		135000
40	Team Lead	44000
40		44000
		251000

44) SQL query to get data in cross-tabulation form from a table

[Create one test table "emp" and add few rows into it as below]

Create table emp (eno number,deptid number,jobtype varchar2(30),salary number)

Insert into emp values (101,10,'Assistant', 10000);
Insert into emp values (102,20,'Analyst', 50000);
Insert into emp values (103,20,'Clerk', 12000);
Insert into emp values (104,30,'Assistant', 20000);
Insert into emp values (105,30,'Manager', 60000);
Insert into emp values (106,30,'Sr analyst', 55000);
Insert into emp values (107,40,'Team Lead', 44000);
Commit;

select deptid,jobtype,sum(salary) from emp group by cube (deptid,jobtype) order by deptid;

Output:

DEPTID	JOBTYPE	SUM(SALARY)
10	Assistant	10000
10		10000
20	Analyst	50000
20	Clerk	12000
20		62000
30	Assistant	20000
30	Manager	60000
30	Sr analyst	55000
30		135000
40	Team Lead	44000
40		44000
	Analyst	50000
	Assistant	30000
	Clerk	12000
	Manager	60000
	Sr analyst	55000

	Team Lead	44000
		251000

45) SQL query to display detail of all employees who earn more than the average salary in their department

[Create one test table "emp" and add few rows into it as below]
Create table emp (eno number,ename varchar2(30),deptid number,jobtype varchar2(30),salary number)

Insert into emp values (101,'Anil',10,'Assistant', 10000);
Insert into emp values (102,'Sunny',20,'Analyst', 50000);
Insert into emp values (103,'Karan',20,'Clerk', 12000);
Insert into emp values (104,'Sam',30,'Assistant', 20000);
Insert into emp values (105,'Peter',30,'Manager', 60000);
Insert into emp values (106,'Lucky',30,'Sr analyst', 55000);
Insert into emp values (107,'Sandy',40,'Team Lead', 44000);
Commit;

select ename,salary,deptid from emp outer where salary > (Select AVG (salary) from emp where deptid=outer.deptid);

Output:

ENAME	SALARY	DEPTID
Sunny	50000	20
Peter	60000	30
Lucky	55000	30

46) SQL query to find employees who have atleast one person reporting to them

[Create one test table "emp" and add few rows into it as below]

Create table emp (eno number,ename varchar2(30),deptid number,jobtype varchar2(30),salary number,manager_id number)

Insert into emp values (101,'Anil',10,'Assistant', 10000,105);
Insert into emp values (102,'Sunny',20,'Analyst', 50000,106);
Insert into emp values (103,'Karan',20,'Clerk', 12000,104);
Insert into emp values (104,'Sam',30,'Assistant', 20000,106);
Insert into emp values (105,'Peter',30,'Manager', 60000,null);
Insert into emp values (106,'Lucky',30,'Sr analyst', 55000,105);

Insert into emp values (107,'Sandy',40,'Team Lead', 44000,106);
Commit;

select eno,ename,jobtype,deptid from emp outer
where exists (Select 'X' from emp where manager_id=outer.eno);

Output:

ENO	ENAME	JOBTYPE	DEPTID
105	Peter	Manager	30
106	Lucky	Sr analyst	30
104	Sam	Assistant	30

47)SQL query to display data in a hierarchical form

[Create one test table "emp" and add few rows into it as below]

Create table emp (eno number,ename varchar2(30),deptid number,jobtype
varchar2(30),salary number,manager_id number)

Insert into emp values (101,'Anil',10,'Assistant', 10000,105);
Insert into emp values (102,'Sunny',20,'Analyst', 50000,106);
Insert into emp values (103,'Karan',20,'Clerk', 12000,104);
Insert into emp values (104,'Sam',30,'Assistant', 20000,106);
Insert into emp values (105,'Peter',30,'Manager', 60000,null);
Insert into emp values (106,'Lucky',30,'Sr analyst', 55000,105);
Insert into emp values (107,'Sandy',40,'Team Lead', 44000,106);
Commit;

Select ename || ' reports to ' || prior ename from emp
Start with eno=105
Connect by prior eno=manager_id;

Output:

HIERARCHICAL_FORM
Peter reports to
Anil reports to Peter
Lucky reports to Peter
Sunny reports to Lucky
Sam reports to Lucky
Karan reports to Sam
Sandy reports to Peter

48) SQL query to create user defined index when creating a table

```
Create table emp
(eno number primary key using index (Create INDEX idx_empid on emp (eno)),
ename varchar2(30),
deptid number,
jobtype varchar2(30),
salary number,
manager_id number);
```

[Where, "idx_empid" is a user-defined Index name]

49) SQL query to create a temporary table

```
Create GLOBAL TEMPORARY TABLE TEMP_EMP (eno number, ename
varchar2(30),esal number)ON COMMIT DELETE ROWS;
```

(OR)

```
Create GLOBAL TEMPORARY TABLE TEMP_EMP (eno number, ename
varchar2(30),esal number)ON COMMIT PRESERVE ROWS;
```

50) SQL query to create a materialized view

```
Create materialized view MV1
Refresh fast with rowid
Enable query rewrite as
Select sales.channel_id C1,
Sum (sales.amount_sold) M1,
Count (*) M2
From sales group by sales.channel_id;
```

51) SQL query to add a default value to a column

```
create table emp
(eno number,
ename varchar2(30),
deptid number,
jobtype varchar2(30),
salary number,
manager_id number,
Hire_date date DEFAULT SYSDATE);
```

[Set System Date as Default date for "Hire_Date" column]

Best 25 Solved Advanced SQL Queries

1) SQL query to fetch first 50 rows from a Table.

    SELECT * FROM employee WHERE ROWNUM < 51;

2) SQL query to fetch 50 random rows from a Table

    SELECT *
     FROM (SELECT *
           FROM employee
         ORDER BY *DBMS_RANDOM.VALUE*)
    WHERE ROWNUM < 51

3) SQL Query to generate Serial/Sequence Number for a Table.

    SELECT sno, empname, salary
     FROM (SELECT empname,
             salary,
               ROW_NUMBER () OVER (ORDER BY salary DESC) sno
          FROM employee);

4) SQL Query to display Even values from a Table.

    Step 1: Create Table "Test":

    CREATE TABLE TEST(A NUMBER);

    Step 2: Insert Rows:

    INSERT INTO TEST VALUES(1);
    INSERT INTO TEST VALUES(15);
    INSERT INTO TEST VALUES(4);
    INSERT INTO TEST VALUES(26);
    INSERT INTO TEST VALUES(497);
    INSERT INTO TEST VALUES(590);
    INSERT INTO TEST VALUES(9826);
    INSERT INTO TEST VALUES(1003);
    INSERT INTO TEST VALUES(333);
    Commit;

Step 3: Final Query:

SELECT * FROM TEST WHERE MOD(A,2)=0;

Output:

A
4
26
590
9826

5) SQL Query to display Odd values from a Table.

Step 1: Create Table "Test":

CREATE TABLE TEST(A NUMBER);

Step 2: Insert Rows:

INSERT INTO TEST VALUES(1);
INSERT INTO TEST VALUES(15);
INSERT INTO TEST VALUES(4);
INSERT INTO TEST VALUES(26);
INSERT INTO TEST VALUES(497);
INSERT INTO TEST VALUES(590);
INSERT INTO TEST VALUES(9826);
INSERT INTO TEST VALUES(1003);
INSERT INTO TEST VALUES(333);
Commit;

Step 3: Final Query:

SELECT * FROM TEST WHERE MOD(A,2)!=0;

Output:

A
1
15
497
1003
333

6) SQL query to display all months between two Dates.

(Suppose Start Date='01-JAN-2014' and End Date='31-JUL-2014')

```
SELECT
TO_CHAR(ADD_MONTHS(TO_DATE('01-JAN-2014', 'DD-MON-YYYY'), ROWNUM -
1),'MON-YY') "DATE"
FROM   DUAL
CONNECT BY
ADD_MONTHS(TO_DATE('01-JAN-2014', 'DD-MON-YYYY')-(EXTRACT(DAY FROM
TO_DATE('01-JAN-2014', 'DD-MON-YYYY')) -1), ROWNUM - 1)
        <= (TO_DATE('31-JUL-2014', 'DD-MON-YYYY'));
```
(OR)

```
select to_char(add_months(to_date('01-JAN-2014','DD-MON-YYYY'),level-1),'MON-
YY') from dual
CONNECT BY
level <= to_char(to_date('31-JUL-2014','DD-MON-YYYY'),'mm')-to_char(to_date('01-
JAN-2014','DD-MON-YYYY'),'mm') +1;
```

Output:

Date
Jan-14
Feb-14
Mar-14
Apr-14
May-14
Jun-14
Jul-14

7) SQL Query to fetch only month's order wise.

Step 1: Create Table "Test":

```
CREATE TABLE TEST (A DATE);
```

Step 2: Insert Rows:

```
INSERT INTO TEST VALUES('01-JAN-12');
INSERT INTO TEST VALUES('11-FEB-12');
INSERT INTO TEST VALUES('21-MAR-12');
INSERT INTO TEST VALUES('30-APR-12');
INSERT INTO TEST VALUES('01-MAY-12');
```

```
INSERT INTO TEST VALUES('02-JUN-12');
INSERT INTO TEST VALUES('06-JUL-12');
INSERT INTO TEST VALUES('10-AUG-12');
INSERT INTO TEST VALUES('30-SEP-12');
INSERT INTO TEST VALUES('28-OCT-12');
INSERT INTO TEST VALUES('18-NOV-12');
INSERT INTO TEST VALUES('31-DEC-12');
COMMIT;
```

Step 3: Final Query:

SELECT TO_CHAR(A,'MON') FROM TEST ORDER BY TO_CHAR(A,'MM');

Output:

TO_CHAR(A,'MON')
JAN
FEB
MAR
APR
MAY
JUN
JUL
AUG
SEP
OCT
NOV
DEC

8) SQL Query to Fetch Numeric Data from String value

    [Suppose String value is: 1DA2SDJD+4567@@##HGSD89HH0]

    select regexp_replace('1DA2SDJD+4567@@##HGSD89HH0','[^0-9]') as "A" FROM dual;

    Output:

A
124567890

9) SQL Query to Fetch Character Data from String value

[Suppose String value is: 1DA2SDJD+4567@@##HGSD89HH0]

select regexp_replace('1DA2SDJD+4567@@##HGSD89HH0','[^A-Z]') as a FROM dual;

Output:

A
DASDJDHGSDHH

10)SQL Query to find duplicate records from a table.

Step 1: Create Table "Employee":

create table employee (empno number, empname varchar2(30), salary number);

Step 2: Insert Rows:

insert into employee values (101,'Anil',20000);
insert into employee values (102,'Ram',30000);
insert into employee values (101,'Anil',20000);
insert into employee values (103,'Karan',25000);
insert into employee values (104,'John',26000);
insert into employee values (105,'Tony',35000);
commit;

Step 3: Final Query:

select empno,empname,salary from employee group by empno,empname,salary having count(empno)>1;

Output:

EMPNO	EMPNAME	SALARY
101	Anil	20000

11)SQL Query to find duplicate data quarter-wise from a table.

Step 1: Create Table "Temp":

```
create table temp (product_id number primary key,stock_no
varchar2(30),price varchar2(30),qty number, creation_date date);
```

Step 2: Insert Rows:

```
insert into temp values (1,'mm001','45.55',5,'22-jan-2012');
insert into temp values (2,'mm002','55.00',6,'2-feb-2012');
insert into temp values (3,'mm003','60.00',8,'20-apr-2012');
insert into temp values (4,'mm001','46.00',5,'29-mar-2012');
insert into temp values (5,'mm004','40.00',9,'2-jul-2012');
insert into temp values (6,'mm003','61.00',65,'3-may-2012');
insert into temp values (7,'mm005','69.00',23,'22-aug-2012');
insert into temp values (8,'mm006','56.00',2,'22-sep-2012');
insert into temp values (9,'mm007','80.00',6,'22-oct-2012');
insert into temp values (10,'mm008','75.00',7,'22-nov-2012');
insert into temp values (11,'mm003','75.00',8,'22-nov-2014');
commit;
```

Step 3: Final Query:

```
SELECT * FROM TEMP WHERE (STOCK_NO,TRUNC(CREATION_DATE,'Q'))
IN(SELECT STOCK_NO,TRUNC(CREATION_DATE,'Q') FROM TEMP GROUP BY
STOCK_NO,TRUNC(CREATION_DATE,'Q') HAVING COUNT( STOCK_NO)>1)
ORDER BY STOCK_NO;
```

Output:

PRODUCT_ID	STOCK_NO	PRICE	QTY	CREATION_DATE
1	MM001	45.55	5	22-Jan-12
4	MM001	46	5	29-Mar-12
3	MM003	60	8	20-Apr-12
6	MM003	61	65	3-May-12

12)SQL Query to find IP Address of a user.

```
Select SYS_CONTEXT('USERENV', 'IP_ADDRESS', 15) AS "IP_ADDRESS" from dual;
```

13) SQL Query to generate queries for Computing, Validating and Rebuilding Indexes.

select 'analyze index TMT.' || object_name || ' compute statistics;' || chr(10) || 'analyze index TMT.' || object_name || ' validate structure;' || chr(10) || 'alter index TMT.' || object_name || ' rebuild online;' from all_objects where owner='TMT' and object_type='INDEX';

[Copy and Execute the result of above Query]

14) SQL Query to compare NULL values in Oracle table.

Step 1: Create two Table "Test1" and "Test2":

CREATE TABLE TEST1 (A NUMBER,B NUMBER);

CREATE TABLE TEST2 (A NUMBER,B NUMBER);

Step 2: Insert Rows:

INSERT INTO TEST1 VALUES (1,25);
INSERT INTO TEST1 VALUES (2,20);
INSERT INTO TEST1 VALUES (3,NULL);
INSERT INTO TEST1 VALUES (4,30);
INSERT INTO TEST1 VALUES (5,NULL);
Commit;

INSERT INTO TEST2 VALUES (1,25);
INSERT INTO TEST2 VALUES (2,NULL);
INSERT INTO TEST2 VALUES (3,20);
INSERT INTO TEST2 VALUES (4,NULL);
INSERT INTO TEST2 VALUES (5,NULL);
Commit;

Step 3: Final Query:

SELECT TEST1.A,TEST1.B,TEST2.B FROM TEST1,TEST2 WHERE TEST1.A=TEST2.A AND NVL(TEST1.B,0)!=NVL(TEST2.B,0);

Output:

A	B	B_1
2	20	
3		20
4	30	

15) SQL query to convert comma separated row data into column.

Step 1: Create Table "Table1":

create table **table1** (**col1** varchar2(500));

Step 2: Insert Rows:

insert into **table1** values ('john, sunny, karan, peter, watson');
commit;

Step 3: Final Query:

with t as (select **col1** from **table1**)
SELECT REGEXP_SUBSTR(**col1**,'[0-9]+|[a-z]+|[A-Z]+',1,**lvl**) "COL1" FROM
(SELECT **col1**,level **lvl** FROM t̲ CONNECT BY level <= LENGTH(**col1**) -
LENGTH(REPLACE(**col1**,'|')) + 1);

(OR)

with t as (select 'john, sunny, karan, peter, watson' from **dual**)
SELECT REGEXP_SUBSTR('john, sunny, karan, peter, watson','[0-9]+|[a-z]+|[A-
Z]+',1,**lvl**) "COL1" FROM
(SELECT 'john, sunny, karan, peter, watson',level **lvl** FROM t CONNECT BY level <=
LENGTH('john, sunny, karan, peter, watson') - LENGTH(REPLACE('john, sunny,
karan, peter, watson',',')) + 1);

Output:

COL1
john
sunny
karan
peter
watson

16) SQL query to convert column data into row data with comma separated.

Step 1: Create Table "Table1":

Create table **table1** (**col1** varchar2(500));

Step 2: Insert Rows:

insert into **table1** values ('john');

insert into **table1** values ('sunny');
insert into **table1** values ('karan');
insert into **table1** values ('peter');
insert into **table1** values ('watson');
commit;

Step 3: Final Query:

SELECT   LISTAGG (col1, ',')
        WITHIN GROUP (ORDER BY ROWID) "COLUMN TO ROW"
            FROM   table1;
Output:

COLUMN TO ROW
john, sunny, karan, peter, watson

17) SQL Query to Find Missing Numbers from a Series in Oracle

Step 1: Create Table "Table1":

Create table test (A number);

Step 2: Insert Rows:

insert into test values (3);
insert into test values (7);
insert into test values (8);
insert into test values (11);
insert into test values (20);
commit;

Step 3: Final Query:

select level "MISSING NUMBERS" from **dual**
   connect by level< 20
     minus
     select A
       from test;

Output:

MISSING NUMBERS
1

2
4
5
6
9
10
12
13
14
15
16
17
18
19

18)SQL query to extract Day, Month and Year from date in Oracle

[Suppose Date Time Field value is "17-Nov-2014 15:35:26"]

Query to fetch day from date:

select extract (day from to_date('17-Nov-2014 15:35:26', 'DD-MON-YYYY HH24:MI:SS')) "DAY" from dual;

Output:

DAY
17

Query to fetch month from date:

select extract (month from to_date('17-Nov-2014 15:35:26', 'DD-MON-YYYY HH24:MI:SS')) "MONTH" from dual;

Output:

MONTH
11

Query to fetch year from date:

select extract (year from to_date('17-Nov-2014 15:35:26', 'DD-MON-YYYY HH24:MI:SS')) "YEAR" from **dual**;

Output:

YEAR
2014

19) SQL query to extract Hours, Minutes and Seconds from date in Oracle

Query to fetch hour from date:

select extract(hour from cast(to_date('17-Nov-2014 15:35:26', 'DD-MON-YYYY HH24:MI:SS')as timestamp)) "HOUR" from **dual**;

Output:

HOUR
15

Query to fetch minutes from date:

select extract(minute from cast(to_date('17-Nov-2014 15:35:26', 'DD-MON-YYYY HH24:MI:SS')as timestamp)) "MINUTES" from **dual**;

Output:

MINUTES
35

Query to fetch seconds from date:

select extract(second from cast(to_date('17-Nov-2014 15:35:26', 'DD-MON-YYYY HH24:MI:SS')as timestamp)) "SECONDS"from **dual**;

Output:

SECONDS
26

20) SQL Query using Recursion in Oracle

Step 1: Create Table "Category":

```
CREATE TABLE CATEGORY
(
  ID      NUMBER Primary Key,
  NAME    VARCHAR2(200 BYTE),
  PARENTID NUMBER References category(ID)
);
```

Step 2: Insert Rows:

```
insert into category values (1,'Test',0);
insert into category values (2,'Test1',1);
insert into category values (3,'Test2',1);
insert into category values (4,'test11',2);
insert into category values (5,'test114',4);
commit;
```

Step 3: Final Query:

```
WITH EntityChildren(id,Name,ParentID) AS
(
SELECT id,Name,ParentID  FROM category WHERE ID = 1
UNION ALL
SELECT e.id,e2.Name ||'-->' || e.Name,e.ParentID FROM category e , EntityChildren
e2 where e.ParentID = e2.id
)
SELECT * from EntityChildren;
```

(OR) Using INNER JOIN Clause

```
WITH EntityChildren(id,Name,ParentID) AS
(
SELECT id,Name,ParentID  FROM category WHERE ID = 1
UNION ALL
SELECT e.id,e2.Name ||'-->' || e.Name,e.ParentID FROM category e INNER JOIN
EntityChildren e2 on e.ParentID = e2.id
)
SELECT * from EntityChildren;
```

Output:

ID	NAME	PARENTID
1	Test	0
2	Test-->Test1	1
3	Test-->Test2	1

4	Test-->Test1-->test11	2
5	Test-->Test1-->test11-->test114	4

21) SQL query to Find 2nd Highest Salary in Oracle.

Step 1: Create Table "Employee":

```
CREATE TABLE EMPLOYEE
(
  EMPNAME  VARCHAR2(100 BYTE),
  SALARY   NUMBER
);
```

Step 2: Insert Rows:

```
insert into Employee values ('John', 500);
insert into Employee values ('Bill', 1000 );
insert into Employee values ('Marry',1000 );
insert into Employee values ('Clinton', 3000 );
insert into Employee values ('Sam', 4000 );
insert into Employee values ('Rita', 5000 );
insert into Employee values ('Sunny', 5000 );
insert into Employee values ('Karan', 6000 );
insert into Employee values ('Danny', 7000 );
insert into Employee values ('Wendy', 7000 );
insert into Employee values ('Mark', 9000 );
Commit;
```

Step 3: Final Query:

Syntax:

```
SELECT * /*This is the outer query part */
FROM Employee Emp1
WHERE (N-1) = ( /* Subquery starts here */
SELECT COUNT(DISTINCT(Emp2.Salary))
FROM Employee Emp2
WHERE Emp2.Salary > Emp1.Salary)
```

Query to find 2nd Highest Salary: (N=2)

```
SELECT * FROM Employee Emp1
WHERE (1) = (SELECT COUNT (DISTINCT (Emp2.Salary))
FROM Employee Emp2
```

WHERE Emp2.Salary > Emp1.Salary);

(OR)

```
select Empname, Salary from (
 select Emp.*,
dense_rank() over (order by Salary Desc) rownumber
from Employee Emp
)
where rownumber = 2;
```

Output:

EMPNAME	SALARY
Danny	7000
Wendy	7000

22) SQL Query to Calculate Tenure Period from Date of Joining.

Step 1: Create Table "Employee":

create table employee (**empno** number, **empname** varchar2(100), **doj** date);

Step 2: Insert Rows:

```
insert into employee values (101, 'Monty', '20-Nov-2012');
insert into employee values (102, 'Binny', '01-Jan-2014');
insert into employee values (103, 'John', '05-Mar-2014');
insert into employee values (104, 'Daniel', '01-Jun-2014');
insert into employee values (105, 'Karan', '21-Jul-2014');
insert into employee values (106, 'Sunny', '14-Sep-2014');
insert into employee values (107, 'Danny', '21-Aug-2014');
Commit;
```

Output Required As:

Employees with tenure of less than 30 days should be shown as "0 to 30 days".
Employees with tenure in between 31-60 days should be shown as "31 to 60 days".
Employees with tenure in between 61-90 days should be shown as "61 to 90 days".
Employees with tenure in between 91-120 days should be shown as "91 to 120 days".
Employees with tenure in between 121-180 days should be shown as "121 to 180 days".

Employees with tenure in between 181-270 days should be shown as "181 to 270 days".

Employees with tenure in between 271-365 days should be shown as "271 to 365 days".

Employees with tenure of greater than 365 days should be shown as "Greater than 365 days".

Step 3: Final Query:

```
select empno,empname,to_date(sysdate,'DD-MON-YYY')
Today_date,doj,round(sysdate-doj) "TENURE" ,
case when to_date(sysdate)- doj<=30 then '0 to 30 days'
when to_date(sysdate)- doj between 31 and 60 then '31 to 60 days'
when to_date(sysdate)- doj between 61 and 90 then '61 to 90 days'
when to_date(sysdate)- doj between 91 and 120 then '91 to 120 days'
when to_date(sysdate)- doj between 121 and 180 then '121 to 180 days'
when to_date(sysdate)- doj between 181 and 270 then '181 to 270 days'
when to_date(sysdate)- doj between 271 and 365 then '271 to 365 days'
else 'Greater than 365 days' end "TENURE PERIOD"
from employee order by empno;
```

Output:

EMPNO	EMPNAME	TODAY_DATE	DOJ	TENURE PERIOD	TENURE
101	Monty	10/11/2014	11/20/2012	691	Greater than 3 days
102	Binny	10/11/2014	1/1/2014	284	271 to 365 da
103	John	10/11/2014	3/5/2014	221	181 to 270 da
104	Daniel	10/11/2014	6/1/2014	133	121 to 180 da
105	Karan	10/11/2014	7/21/2014	83	61 to 90 day
106	Sunny	10/11/2014	9/14/2014	28	0 to 30 day
107	Danny	10/11/2014	8/21/2014	52	31 to 60 day

23) SQL query to calculate number of Days, Hours, Minutes and Seconds between two dates

[Suppose start date is '01-Jan-2014' and end date is '31-Jul-2014']

Number of Days between two dates:
```
select to_date('31-Jul-2014','dd-mon-yyyy') - to_date('01-Jan-2014','dd-mon-yyyy')
"Number of Days" from dual;
```

Output:

Number of Days
211

Number of Hours between two dates:
[Suppose start date is '30-Jul-2014 13:00:00' and end date is '31-Jul-2014 06:00:00']

select ((to_date('31-JUL-2014 06:00:00','dd-mon-yyyy hh24:mi:ss') - to_date('30-JUL-2014 13:00:00','dd-mon-yyyy hh24:mi:ss'))*24) "Number of Hours" from dual;

Output:

Number of Hours
17

Number of Minutes between two dates:
[Suppose start date is '31-Jul-2014 05:00:00' and end date is '31-Jul-2014 06:00:00']

select ((to_date('31-JUL-2014 06:00:00','dd-mon-yyyy hh24:mi:ss') - to_date('31-JUL-2014 05:00:00','dd-mon-yyyy hh24:mi:ss'))*24*60) "Number of Minutes" from dual;

Output:

Number of Minutes
60

Number of Seconds between two dates:
[Suppose start date is '31-Jul-2014 06:30:05' and end date is '31-Jul-2014 06:30:30']

select ((to_date('31-JUL-2014 06:30:30','dd-mon-yyyy hh24:mi:ss') - to_date('31-JUL-2014 06:30:05','dd-mon-yyyy hh24:mi:ss'))*24*60*60) "Number of Seconds" from dual;

Output:

Number of Seconds
25

24) SQL query to find week in number for a month and a year

Step 1: Create Table "Test":
create table test (COL_DATE Date);

Step 2: Insert Rows:

insert into test values('01-Jan-2014');
insert into test values('11-Mar-2014');
insert into test values('19-Sep-2014');
insert into test values('20-Nov-2014');
insert into test values('31-Dec-2014');
Commit;

Step 3: Final Query:

Week of a month:

select COL_DATE,to_Char(COL_DATE,'MON-YYYY')
Month_Year,to_char(COL_DATE,'W') Week_Number,
case when to_char(COL_DATE,'W')=1 then 'Week 1'
when to_char(COL_DATE,'W')=2 then 'Week 2'
when to_char(COL_DATE,'W')=3 then 'Week 3'
when to_char(COL_DATE,'W')=4 then 'Week 4'
when to_char(COL_DATE,'W')=5 then 'Week 5'
else null end Week_of_Month
from test;

(OR)

select COL_DATE,to_Char(COL_DATE,'MON-YYYY')
Month_Year,to_char(COL_DATE,'W') Week_Number,
'Week' || ' ' ||to_char(COL_DATE,'W') Week_of_Month
from test;

Output:

COL_DATE	MONTH_YEAR	WEEK_NUMBER	WEEK_OF_MONTH
1/1/2014	Jan-14	1	Week 1
3/11/2014	Mar-14	2	Week 2
9/19/2014	Sep-14	3	Week 3
11/20/2014	Nov-14	3	Week 3
12/31/2014	Dec-14	5	Week 5

Week of a Year

```
select COL_DATE,to_Char(COL_DATE,'MON-YYYY')
Month_Year,to_char(COL_DATE,'WW') Week_Number,
'Week' || ' ' ||to_char(COL_DATE,'WW') Week_of_Year from test;
```

Output:

COL_DATE	MONTH_YEAR	WEEK_NUMBER	WEEK_OF_YEAR
1/1/2014	Jan-14	1	Week 01
3/11/2014	Mar-14	10	Week 10
9/19/2014	Sep-14	38	Week 38
11/20/2014	Nov-14	47	Week 47
12/31/2014	Dec-14	53	Week 53

25) SQL query to remove line feed from value in oracle.

[Suppose we have one table "TESTING" with column "FIELD_VALUE"]. Following value is saved in the "FIELD_VALUE" column with line break as shown below:

"This is a test data

to check line feed."

To remove line feed follow following query:

```
UPDATE TESTING SET FIELD_VALUE=REPLACE (REPLACE (FIELD_VALUE, CHR (13),''), CHR (10),'');
```

Output:

Field_Value
This is a test data to check line feed.

Best 120 SQL and PL/SQL Tips

1. Zero is a number and a Space is a character.

2. Character strings and date values are enclosed in single quotation marks.

3. Character values are case sensitive and date values are format sensitive.

4. The default date format is DD-MON-RR. Oracle database stores date in a format: Century, year, month, day, hours, minutes and seconds.

5. An Alias cannot be used in the WHERE clause.

6. The symbol ! = and ^= also represents to not equal to condition.

7. Values specified with the BETWEEN condition are inclusive.

8. The IN condition is also called membership condition.

9. The IN condition can be used with any data type.

10. A NULL value cannot be equal (=) or unequal to any value.

11. NULL values are displayed last for ascending sequences and first for descending

12. Column Alias can be used in the ORDER BY clause.

13. Sysdate is a function that does not contain any argument but return current database server date and time.

14. Database stores dates as Numbers, so arithmetic operators such as addition and subtraction can be performed on dates.

15. All Group Functions ignores null values. To substitutes a value for null values, use the NVL, NVL2, or COALESCE functions.

16. The oracle server implicitly sorts the result set in ascending order when using a "Group By" clause. To override this default ordering, DESC can be used in an "Order By" clause.

17. MIN and MAX functions can be used for any data type.

18. AVG, SUM, VARIANCE, and STDDEV functions can be used only with Numeric data types.

19. You cannot use a column alias in the GROUP BY clause.

20. All columns in the SELECT list that are not in group functions must be in the GROUP BY clause.

21. The GROUP BY column does not have to be in the SELECT list.

22. To restrict groups use HAVING clause not WHERE clause.

23. Don't use Group functions in the Where clause.

24. Using the Table prefixes (alias) with the column names improves Performance, because it tells the oracle server exactly where to find the columns. It also helps to keep SQL code smaller, therefore using less memory.

25. A condition involving an Outer Join cannot use IN and OR operator.

26. The statement with the values clause adds only one row at a time to a table.

27. You can use a subquery in place of the table name in to INTO clause of the INSERT statement.

28. When creating a table by using a subquery, the integrity rules are not passed on to the new table, only the column data type definitions are passed.

29. When you add a new column in a table using ALTER command, than the new column become the last column in that table.

30. During modifying a column you can increase the width of a numeric or character column.

31. During modifying a column you can decrease the width of a column only if the column contains only null values or if the table has no rows.

32. During modifying a column you can change the data type only if the column contains null values

33. You can convert a CHAR column to the VARCHAR2 data type or convert a VARCHAR2 column to the CHAR data type only if the column contains null values or if you do not change the size.

34. A change to the default value of a column affects only subsequent insertions to the table.

35. Using the ALTER TABLE statement, only one column can be dropped at time and the table must have at least one column remaining in it after it is altered.

36. You can add a comment of up to 2000 bytes about a column, table, view or snapshot by using the COMMENT statement.

37. You can define any constraint at the Table level except NOT NULL which is defined only at column level.

38. Without the ON DELETE CASCADE or the ON DELETE SET NULL options, the Row in the parent table cannot be deleted if it is referenced in the child table.

39. You can add a NOT NULL constraint to an existing column by using the MODIFY clause of the ALTER TABLE statement.

40. You can define a NOT NULL column only if the table is empty or if the column has a value for every row

41. A View can be modifying by using the CREATE or REPLACE option.

42. When you drop a table, corresponding indexes are also dropped.

43. More Indexes on a table does not mean faster queries. Each DML operations that are committed on a table with indexes must be updated. The more indexes you have associated with a table, the more effort the oracle server must make to update all the indexes after a DML operation.

44. You cannot modify indexes. To change an Index, you must drop it and the recreates it.

45. If you drop a table, Indexes and Constraints are automatically dropped but Views and Sequences remains.

46. A user can have access to several Roles and several users can be assigned the same Role. Roles are typically created for database application.

47. An owner of a table can grant access to all users by using the PUBLIC keyword.

48. Privileges cannot be granted on remote objects.

49. PL/SQL Engine processes the entire PL/SQL block and filters out the SQL and procedural Statements separately, this reduces the amount of work that is sent to the oracle server and the number of memory cursors that are required.

50. PL/SQL code can be stored in oracle server as subprograms and can be referenced by any number of applications that are connected to the database.

51. In PL/SQL, an error is called an Exception.

52. If using NOT NULL or CONSTANT with variable declaration, you must assign a value to it.

53. To assign a value into a variable from a database, use SELECT or FETCH statements.

54.A slash (/) runs the PL/SQL block in a script file or in some tools such as iSQL*Plus.

55. DECODE and Group Functions (Avg, Sum, Min, Max, Count, Stddev, and Variance) are not available in procedural statements. They can be used in an SQL statement in a PL/SQL block.

56. An exception section can contain nested blocks.

57. The Scope of the identifier is that region of a program unit (block, subprogram, or package) from which you can reference the identifier.

58. PL/SQL does not directly support DDL statements such as Create, Alter, and Drop table.

59. PL/SQL does not directly support DCL statements such as GRANT and REVOKE.

60. PL/SQL supports DML (Insert, Update, and Delete) and Transaction control commands of SQL (Commit, Rollback, Savepoint)

61. Select statements within PL/SQL block must return one and only one row. A query that returns more than one row (TOO_MANY_ROWS) or no row (NO_DATA_FOUND) generates an error.

62. PL/SQL does not return an error if a DML statement does not affect any rows in the underlying table, however if a SELECT statement does not retrieve any rows PL/SQL returns an exception.

63. SQL%ISOPEN always evaluates to FALSE because PL/SQL closes the implicit cursors immediately after they are executed.

64. The PL/SQL program opens a cursor, processes rows returned by a query and then closes the cursor. The cursor makes the current position in the Active set.

65. Declare variables before the cursor declaration.

66. If the query returns no rows, no exception is raised.

67. You cannot reference cursor attributes directly in a SQL statement.

68. Before the first fetch %NOTFOUND evaluates to Null. So if Fetch never executes successfully, the Loop is never exited, that is because the EXIT WHEN statement. Executes

only if it's WHEN condition is true. To be safe, use the following EXIT statement: EXIT WHEN emp_cursor%NOTFOUND or emp_cursor%NOTFOUND is Null.

69. When the same cursor is referenced repeatedly we can pass parameters to the cursor. We can also use cursor for loop with parameters.

70. A block always terminates when PL/SQL raises an exception.

71. Exception cannot appear in assignment statements or SQL statements.

72. You cannot use SQLCODE and SQLERRM directly in a SQL statement. Instead, you must assign their values to local variables, and then use the variables in the SQL statement.

73. The keyword DECLARE that is used to indicate the starting of the declaration section in anonymous blocks is not used with the subprograms (Procedures or functions).

74. There must be at least one statement existing in the executable section, there must be atleast A NULL statement that is considered an executable statement.

75. You cannot reference host or bind variables in the PL/SQL block of a stored Procedure.

76. You cannot restrict the size of the data type in the parameters of the subprograms.

77. You must declare the subprogram in the declaration section of the block and must be the last item after all the other program items. For example: A variable declared after the end of the subprogram, before the begin of the procedure, will cause the compilation error.

78. A Function must have a Return Clause in the Header and at least one Return Statement in the executable section.

79. Return data type in function declaration must not include a size specification.

80. You cannot reference host or bind variables in the PL/SQL block of a stored Function.

81. Although multiple Return statements are allowed in a function (usually within an IF statement) only one Return statement is executed.

82. It is a good programming practice to assign a return value to a variable and use a single return Statement in the executable section of the code. There can be a return statement in the exception Section of the program also.

83. A Function may accept one or many parameter, but must return a single value.

84. Although the three parameters modes (IN, OUT, INOUT) can be used with any subprogram, avoid Using the OUT and INOUT modes with Functions.

85. Anywhere a built-in function can be placed, a user-defined function can be placed as well.

86. Only stored functions are callable from SQL statements. Stored Procedures cannot be called.

87. Functions that are callable from SQL expressions cannot contain OUT and INOUT parameters, other functions can contain parameters wit these modes but it is not recommended.

88. A Procedure containing one OUT Parameter can rewritten as a function containing a RETURN Statement.

89. Package cannot be invoked, parameterized or nested.

90. Package Specification and Body are stored separately in the database but must have the same name.

91. Define the Package Specification before the Body.

92. A Package Specification can exist without a package Body, but a package Body cannot exist without a package Specification.

93. It is quite common in the package body to see all private variables and subprograms defined first and the public subprograms defined last.

94. If a Specification declares only types, constants, variables, exceptions and call specifications, the package body is unnecessary. However, the body can still be used to initialize items declared in the package specification.

95. Changes to the package specification require recompilation of each referencing subprogram. So place few construct as possible in a package specification.

96. Only local or packaged subprograms can be overloaded. You cannot overload stand-alone.

97. Most built-in functions are overloaded. For ex: TO_CHAR function of standard package.

98. PL/SQL does not allow forward references; you must declare an identifier before using it. Therefore, a program must be declared before calling it.

99. The excessive use of Triggers can result in complex inter-dependencies, which may be difficult to maintain in large applications. Only use Triggers when necessary and beware of recursive and cascading effects.

100. If the logic for the Trigger is very lengthy, create stored procedures with the logic and invoke them in the Trigger body using CALL statement. There is no semicolon at the end of call statement.

101. Note that database triggers fire for every user each time the event occurs for which the Trigger is created.

102. The size of a Trigger cannot be more than 32K.

103. Using column names along with the Update clause in the Trigger improves performance, because the Trigger fires only when the particular column is updated and thus avoids unintended firing when any other column is updated.

104. You can combine several Triggering events into one by taking advantage of a special conditional predicates INSERTING, UPDATING, DELETING with the Trigger body.

105. The OLD and NEW qualifiers are available only in ROW Triggers and prefix these qualifiers with a colon (:) in every SQL and PL/SQL statement.

106. There is no colon (:) prefix if the qualifiers are referenced in the WHEN restricting ROW Trigger can decrease the performance if you do a lot of updates on larger tables.

107. When you specify ON SCHEMA, the Trigger fires for the specific user, if you specify ON DATABASE, the Trigger fires for all users.

108. A Table is not considered Mutating for statement Triggers.

109. Statements in the Trigger Body operate under the privilege of the Trigger owner, not the Trigger user.

110. If the Package body changes and the Package specification does not changes, the stand-alone Procedure referencing a package construct remains valid.

111. If the package specification changes, the outside procedure referencing a package construct is invalidated, as is the package body.

112. If a Stand-alone procedure referenced within the package changes, the entire package body is invalidated, but the package specification remains valid. Therefore, it is recommended that you bring the procedure into the package.

113. Dynamic SQL supports all the SQL data types but does not supports PL/SQL specific types except PL/SQL record.

114. You can use the INTO clause for a single-row query, but you must use OPEN-FOR, FETCH and CLOSE for a multi row query.

115. The oracle 9i server performs implicit conversion between CLOB and VARCHAR2 data types. The other implicit conversions between LOB's are not possible. Foe ex: if the user creates a table T with a CLOB column and a table S with a BLOB column, the data is not directly transferable between these two columns.

116. Modify View using "Create or Replace" clause.

117. The sequence must be dropped and re-created to restart the sequence at a different number.

118. You can rename table as well as column names using "rename" clause.

119. The maximum number of columns in a table can be 1000.

120. The file name has a maximum size of 255 characters.

www.ingramcontent.com/pod-product-compliance
Lightning Source LLC
Chambersburg PA
CBHW061025050326
40689CB00012B/2705